808.83
FAI

+ 264 . 284

Four Modern Story-Tellers

KT-489-163

-2. FEB. 1989

Edited by

M.T. FAIN

903757

HEREWARD COLLEGE OF FURTHER EDUCATION

BRAMSTON   CRESCENT

COVENTRY   CV4 9SW

3230

HEINEMANN EDUCATIONAL BOOKS

LONDON

Heinemann Educational Books Ltd
LONDON EDINBURGH MELBOURNE AUCKLAND TORONTO
HONG KONG SINGAPORE KUALA LUMPUR NEW DELHI
NAIROBI JOHANNESBURG LUSAKA IBADAN
KINGSTON

ISBN 0 435 13200 8

Preface, Biographies and Suggestions for
Further Reading © M. T. Fain 1977
First published 1977
Reprinted 1978

Published by
Heinemann Educational Books Ltd
48 Charles Street, London W1X 8AH
Printed and bound in Great Britain by
Morrison & Gibb Ltd, London and Edinburgh

Contents

Preface

With few exceptions anthologies of short stories have been of two kinds: single-author collections, and miscellanies by many authors sometimes with a central theme. Both types have their limitations. The first lacks variety whereas the second often has it to excess. For this volume I have avoided these extremes by selecting some of the finest stories written by four modern masters of the form.

I have tried to include in the space available a representative selection from the work of each writer. All the stories are within reach of the average candidate for GCE Ordinary Level English Literature and I have borne in mind the interests of the teenage reader. Nevertheless the stories were originally written for adults and the material is handled in an honest and mature way.

The technique of each author is very different and expresses an individual attitude to life often drawn from very personal experiences. The arrangement of this anthology, however, provides an opportunity for a study in some depth of each writer. Although it is not thematic, the same subjects, for example courtship and marriage, love and liberty, youth and old-age, often recur in different guises and there are opportunities for rewarding comparative study.

Modern writers have drawn attention to the shrinking market for short stories and a symptom of this decline can be seen by comparing the financial rewards which Scott Fitzgerald received with those available today. The future of the short story is, however, assured as a literary enterprise if not as an economic proposition. It is a challenging and attractive form in which to write and has always been characterised by a wide variety of form and style. The stories in this volume vary from the profoundly serious to the mildly entertaining but they all make an impact within a brief space. Short stories of quality will endure because of their capacity to stimulate thought, to sharpen the reader's understanding and awareness of life, and to give lasting pleasure.

M.T. FAIN

F. Scott Fitzgerald (1896-1940)

Scott Fitzgerald wrote his first short story at the age of thirteen. It was published in his school magazine at St Paul, Minnesota in the American Middle-West. Between then and his early death at the age of forty-four he published some one hundred and sixty short stories in addition to sketches, essays and autobiographical pieces. Even in the final year of his life when Fitzgerald was sick and frequently bedridden he produced the seventeen *Pat Hobby Stories* which were printed in *Esquire* magazine and finally published in book form in 1962. Witty and sympathetic though these stories are, some readers might wish that the time could have been spent on his final, and possibly greatest novel, *The Last Tycoon,* which was never completed. Throughout his life Fitzgerald never completely freed himself from the lucrative magazine market, and many of his lasting successes were achieved in spite of it rather than with its help. Both *The Jelly-Bean* and *Outside the Cabinet Maker's* were turned down by *The Saturday Evening Post,* Fitzgerald's main outlet, although during the twenties up to $4000 was paid for far inferior stories. The former has its moments of hilarity but the sad ending and note of pathos departed from the formula which the editors required.

Much of Fitzgerald's writing is in some sense autobiographical. As he says in the essay about the problems of writing, entitled 'One Hundred False Starts' (1933): 'Whether it's something that happened twenty years ago or only yesterday, I must start out with an emotion—one that's close to me and that I can understand.' This emotional sincerity is the foundation for much of Fitzgerald's fiction and its personal quality has a direct appeal for the reader. It was not, however, what was wanted in Hollywood, where Fitzgerald spent the last years of his life working as a script-writer. Moving pictures required action; emotion was an unsought

1

refinement. Compare Fitzgerald's stories with those of Somerset Maugham where the ¦ story-line is predominant, *Winter Cruise* for example which appears on p.71. There is little doubt which provide the best source material for film scripts.

These conflicts between what Fitzgerald wrote best and what the public expected of him explain much of the frustration and bitterness which he felt in later life. A further difficulty was his adoption by fashionable society as the poet and shining example of the 'Jazz Age' with its extravagance and permissiveness. It was a role which he did not adapt to immediately, as he explains in *My Lost City* (1932). 'I was pushed into the position not only of spokesman for the time but of the typical product of that same moment.' His new wife, Zelda Sayre, was from Montgomery, Alabama; he was from the Mid-West. They were both strangers to the glitter and sophistication of Manhattan: 'We felt like small children in a great bright unexplored barn.' The overnight success of his first novel, *This Side of Paradise*, for all its youthful imperfections, had made him a national hero, and this was no easy position for the twenty-four-year-old author to sustain.

Fitzgerald had become acquainted with the South during his trips to the Sayre household in Montgomery, Alabama. He also spent several weeks early in 1920 in New Orleans trying unsuccessfully to work on his second novel, while he waited for *This Side of Paradise* to be published. Something of the impression it made upon him is revealed by Anthony Patch, the hero of his second novel, *The Beautiful and Damned*. 'Anthony, loitering along through the warm dusk, felt for the first time in years the slow, erotic breath of the South, imminent in the hot softness of the air, in the pervasive lull of thought and time.' This is the setting for Anthony's first meeting with Dorothy Raycroft and it is against this same background that Jim Powell falls hopelessly in love with Nancy Lamar in *The Jelly-Bean*. She has all the qualities which, taken together, earned the title 'flapper' during the next decade. She is beautiful and reckless, hard and yet sensitive, selfish and yet generous and above all immensely sympathetic. Compare her with her friend Sally Carrol Happer, the heroine of *The Ice Palace* published in the same year. Compare her too with Jim Powell. It is of course an impossible match and yet, for all his 'loafing', Jim is a proud, independent person descended from a once rich and influential family. Although a social embarrassment to Clark Darrow, he nevertheless retains his friendship. The party has, however, to end sometime and when it does Nancy is married (to Merritt safety razors!). Jim's pathetic and yet honourable resolution 'to be like a gentleman' has come too late and he returns to his old ways. Although an early work, *The Jelly-Bean* is a remarkably sensitive and equally unsentimentalised view of the South, which exhibits Fitzgerald's great, natural flair for handling the short-story form.

Outside the Cabinet-Maker's is an example of an incident, superficially unremarkable, into which the author infuses an unexpected depth of feeling. It is a popular device with short-story-writers since the incident provides a clear narrative line and a ready-made conclusion. Fitzgerald also makes use of a story within a story which enhances the narrative interest. The couple are arranging to have a doll's house built for their daughter. The man feels full of love for her at this beautiful age but when he tries to tell her this she only 'smiles politely'. The fairy story, which although it captivates the girl and amuses the reader rather bores its narrator, is a hopeless attempt to translate the feelings of an adult into the language of a child. It also expresses the father's lament for the time when life was full of unexplained mystery, and sounds perhaps the central theme of much of Fitzgerald's fiction: the loss of youth with all its loves and joys.

In the third and final story Fitzgerald exposes the sad irony of the good-looking couple who 'have so much in common' and he incidentally introduces a fascinating debate on marriage. The title phrase is one which appears to have haunted him for some years. In *This Side of Paradise* Isabella, Amory's first and juvenile love of his Princeton years, has a similar thought during a party from which they retire to be alone in the den. 'She was conscious that they were a handsome pair, and seemed to belong distinctively in this seclusion, while lesser lights fluttered and chattered downstairs.' The relationship, however, soon ended. Nelson and Nicole in *One Trip Abroad* (1930) are described as a 'handsome couple' before they 'lose peace and love and health, one after the other'. The phrase is, of course, a cliché and the story is rich in irony. Apart from the central theme that Stuart and Helen are so well matched that they spend their lives competing and trying to outdo each other, there is the further twist at the end of the story where Stuart compares his apparent failure with Teddy Van Beck's professional success. Stuart doesn't know the final achievement which is awaiting him and is not qualified to assess his life fairly. After all how easy is it for Teddy, witty, arrogant and artistic, to live with a domesticated woman who has none of these qualities and who 'held none of the world's dark magic for him'? Is it the perfect solution as he maintains or is it simply a compromise which enables him to get on with his work?

The Jelly-Bean

JIM POWELL was a Jelly-bean. Much as I desire to make him an appealing character, I feel that it would be unscrupulous to deceive you on that point. He was a bred-in-the-bone, dyed-in-the-wool, ninety-nine and three-quarters per cent Jelly-bean and he grew lazily all during Jelly-bean season, which is every season, down in the land of the Jelly-beans well below the Mason-Dixon line.

Now if you call a Memphis man a Jelly-bean he will quite possibly pull a long sinewy rope from his hip pocket and hang you to a convenient telegraph pole. If you call a new Orleans man a Jelly-bean he will probably grin and ask you who is taking your girl to the Mardi Gras ball.* The particular Jelly-bean patch which produced the protagonist of this history lies somewhere between the two—a little city of forty thousand that has dozed sleepily for forty thousand years in southern Georgia, occasionally stirring in its slumbers and muttering something about a war that took place sometime, somewhere, and that everyone else has forgotten long ago.

Jim was a Jelly-bean. I write that again because it has such a pleasant sound—rather like the beginning of a fairy story—as if Jim were nice. It somehow gives me a picture of him with a round, appetising face and all sorts of leaves and vegetables grow-

*In Memphis, Tennessee, which is some 400 miles north of New Orleans and outside the Jelly-bean belt, the term would be considered an insult.

4

ing out of his cap. But Jim was long and thin and bent at the waist from stooping over pool-tables, and he was what might have been known in the indiscriminating North as a corner loafer. 'Jelly-bean' is the name throughout the undissolved Confederacy for one who spends his life conjugating the verb to idle in the first person singular—I am idling, I have idled, I will idle.

Jim was born in a white house on a green corner. It had four weather-beaten pillars in front and a great amount of lattice-work in the rear that made a cheerful criss-cross background for a flowery sun-drenched lawn. Originally the dwellers in the white house had owned the ground next door and next door to that and next door to that, but this had been so long ago that even Jim's father scarcely remembered it. He had, in fact, thought it a matter of so little moment that when he was dying from a pistol wound got in a brawl he neglected even to tell little Jim, who was five years old and miserably frightened. The white house became a boarding-house run by a tight-lipped lady from Macon, whom Jim called Aunt Mamie and detested with all his soul.

He became fifteen, went to high school, wore his hair in black snarls, and was afraid of girls. He hated his home where four women and one old man prolonged an interminable chatter from summer to summer about what lots the Powell place had originally included and what sort of flowers would be out next. Sometimes the parents of little girls in town, remembering Jim's mother and fancying a resemblance in the dark eyes and hair, invited him to parties, but parties made him shy and he much preferred sitting on a disconnected axle in Tilly's Garage, rolling the bones or exploring his mouth endlessly with a long straw. For pocket money, he picked up odd jobs, and it was due to this that he stopped going to parties. At his third party little Marjorie Haight had whispered indiscreetly and within hearing distance that he was a boy who brought the groceries sometimes. So instead of the two-step and polka, Jim had learned to throw any number he desired on the dice and had listened to spicy tales of all the shootings that had occurred in the surrounding country during the past fifty years.

He became eighteen. The war broke out and he enlisted as a gob* and polished brass in the Charleston Navy-yard for a year.

*A slang term for a member of the U.S. Navy.

Then, by way of variety, he went North and polished brass in the Brooklyn Navy-yard for a year.

When the war was over he came home. He was twenty-one, his trousers were too short and too tight. His buttoned shoes were long and narrow. His tie was an alarming conspiracy of purple and pink marvellously scrolled, and over it were two blue eyes faded like a piece of very good old cloth long exposed to the sun.

In the twilight of one April evening when a soft grey had drifted down along the cottonfields and over the sultry town, he was a vague figure leaning against a board fence, whistling and gazing at the moon's rim above the lights of Jackson Street. His mind was working persistently on a problem that had held his attention for an hour. The Jelly-bean had been invited to a party.

Back in the days when all the boys had detested all the girls, Clark Darrow and Jim had sat side by side in school. But, while Jim's social aspirations had died in the oily air of the garage, Clark had alternately fallen in and out of love, gone to college, taken to drink, given it up, and, in short, become one of the best beaux of the town. Nevertheless Clark and Jim had retained a friendship that, though casual, was perfectly definite. That afternoon Clark's ancient Ford had slowed up beside Jim, who was on the sidewalk and, out of a clear sky, Clark had invited him to a party at the country club. The impulse that made him do this was no stranger than the impulse which made Jim accept. The latter was probably an unconscious ennui, a half-frightened sense of adventure. And now Jim was soberly thinking it over.

He began to sing, drumming his long foot idly on a stone block in the sidewalk till it wobbled up and down in time to the low throaty tune:

> One mile from Home in Jelly-bean town,
> Lives Jeanne, the Jelly-bean Queen.
> She loves her dice and treats 'em nice;
> No dice would treat her mean.

He broke off and agitated the sidewalk to a bumpy gallop. 'Doggone!' he muttered, half aloud.

They would all be there—the old crowd, the crowd to which, by right of the white house, sold long since, and the portrait of the officer in grey over the mantel, Jim should have belonged. But that crowd had grown up together into a tight little set as gradually as the girls' dresses had lengthened inch by inch, as definitely as the boys' trousers had dropped suddenly to their ankles. And to that society of first names and dead puppy-loves Jim was an outsider—a running mate of poor whites. Most of the men knew him, condescendingly; he tipped his hat to three or four girls. That was all.

When the dusk had thickened into a blue setting for the moon, he walked through the hot, pleasantly pungent town to Jackson Street. The stores were closing and the last shoppers were drifting homeward, as if borne on the dreamy revolution of a slow merry-go-round. A street fair farther down made a brilliant alley of vari-coloured booths and contributed a blend of music to the night—an oriental dance on a calliope, a melancholy bugle in front of a freak show, a cheerful rendition of 'Back Home in Tennessee' on a hand-organ.

The Jelly-bean stopped in a store and bought a collar. Then he sauntered along towards Soda Sam's, where he found the usual three or four cars of a summer evening parked in front and the little darkies running back and forth with sundaes and lemonades.

'Hello, Jim.'

It was a voice at his elbow—Joe Ewing sitting in an automobile with Marylyn Wade. Nancy Lamar and a strange man were in the back seat.

The Jelly-bean tipped his hat quickly.

'Hi, Joe—' then, after an almost imperceptible pause—'How y' all?'

Passing, he ambled on towards the garage where he had a room upstairs. His 'How y' all' had been said to Nancy Lamar, to whom he had not spoken in fifteen years.

Nancy had a mouth like a remembered kiss and shadowy eyes and blue-black hair inherited from her mother, who had been born in Budapest. Jim passed her often in the street, walking small-boy fashion with her hands in her pockets, and he knew that with her inseparable Sally Carrol Happer she had left a trail of broken hearts from Atlanta to New Orleans.

For a few fleeting moments Jim wished he could dance. Then he laughed and as he reached his door began to sing softly to himself:

> Her Jelly Roll can twist your soul,
> Her eyes are big and brown,
> She's the Queen of the Queens of the Jelly-Beans—
> My Jeanne of Jelly-bean Town.

II

At nine-thirty Jim and Clark met in front of Soda Sam's and started for the Country Club in Clark's Ford.

'Jim,' asked Clark casually, as they rattled through the jasmine-scented night, 'how do you keep alive?'

The Jelly-bean paused, considered.

'Well,' he said finally, 'I got a room over Tilly's garage. I help him some with the cars in the afternoon an' he gives it to me free. Sometimes I drive one of his taxis and pick up a little thataway. I get fed up doin' that regular though.'

'That all?'

'Well, when there's a lot of work I help him by the day—Saturdays usually—and then there's one main source of revenue I don't generally mention. Maybe you don't recollect I'm about the champion crap-shooter of this town. They make me shoot from a cup now because once I get the feel of a pair of dice they just roll for me.'

Clark grinned appreciatively.

'I never could learn to set 'em so's they'd do what I wanted. Wish you'd shoot with Nancy Lamar some day and take all her money away from her. She will roll 'em with the boys and she loses more than her daddy can afford to give her. I happen to know she sold a good ring last month to pay a debt.'

The Jelly-bean was noncommital.

'The white house on Elm Street still belong to you?'

Jim shook his head.

'Sold. Got a pretty good price, seein' it wasn't in a good part of town no more. Lawyer told me to put it into Liberty bonds. But Aunt Mamie got so she didn't have no sense, so it takes all the interest to keep her up at Great Farms Sanatorium.'

'Hm.'

'I got an old uncle up-state an' I reckon I kin go up there if ever I get sure enough pore. Nice farm, but not enough niggers around to work it. He's asked me to come up and help him, but I don't guess I'd take much to it. Too doggone lonesome—' He broke off suddenly. 'Clark, I want to tell you I'm much obliged to you for askin' me out, but I'd be a lot happier if you'd just stop the car right here an' let me walk back into town.'

'Shucks!' Clark grunted. 'Do you good to step out. You don't have to dance—just get out there on the floor and shake.'

'Hold on,' exclaimed Jim uneasily, 'Don't you go leadin' me up to any girls and leavin' me there so I'll have to dance with 'em.'

Clark laughed.

' 'Cause,' continued Jim desperately, 'without you swear you won't do that I'm agoin' to get out right here an' my good legs goin' carry me back to Jackson Street.'

They agreed after some argument that Jim, unmolested by females, was to view the spectacle from a secluded settee in the corner, where Clark would join him whenever he wasn't dancing.

So ten o'clock found the Jelly-bean with his legs crossed and his arms conservatively folded, trying to look casually at home and politely uninterested in the dancers. At heart he was torn between overwhelming self-consciousness and an intense curiosity as to all that went on around him. He saw the girls emerge one by one from the dressing-room, stretching and pluming them-selves like bright birds, smiling over their powdered shoulders at the chaperones, casting a quick glance around to take in the room and, simultaneously, the room's reaction to their entrance—and then, again like birds, alighting and nestling in the sober arms of their waiting escorts. Sally Carrol Happer, blonde and lazy-eyed, appeared clad in her favourite pink and blinking like an awakened rose. Marjorie Haight, Marylyn Wade, Harriet Cary, all the girls he had seen loitering down Jackson Street by noon, now, curled and brilliantined and delicately tinted for the overhead lights, were miraculously strange Dresden figures of pink and blue and red and gold, fresh from the shop and not yet fully dried.

He had been there half an hour, totally uncheered by Clark's jovial visits, which were each one accompanied by a 'Hello, old boy, how you making out?' and a slap at his knee. A dozen males had spoken to him or stopped for a moment beside him, but he knew that they were each one surprised at finding him there and fancied that one or two were even slightly resentful. But at half past ten his embarrassment suddenly left him and a pull of breathless interest took him completely out of himself— Nancy Lamar had come out of the dressing-room.

She was dressed in yellow organdie, a costume of a hundred cool corners, with three tiers of ruffles and a big bow in black, until she shed black and yellow around her in a sort of phosphorescent lustre. The Jelly-bean's eyes opened wide and a lump rose in his throat. For a minute she stood beside the door until her partner hurried up. Jim recognized him as the stranger who had been with her in Joe Ewing's car that afternoon. He saw her arms set akimbo and say something in a low voice, and laugh. The man laughed too and Jim experienced the quick pang of a weird new kind of pain. Some ray had passed between the pair, a shaft of beauty from that sun that had warmed him a moment since. The Jelly-bean felt suddenly like a weed in a shadow.

A minute later Clark approached him, bright-eyed and glowing.

'Hi, old man,' he cried with some lack of originality. 'How you making out?'

Jim replied that he was making out as well as could be expected.

'You come along with me,' commanded Clark. 'I've got something that'll put an edge on the evening.'

Jim followed him awkwardly across the floor and up the stairs to the locker-room where Clark produced a flask of nameless yellow liquid.

'Good old corn.'

Ginger ale arrived on a tray. Such potent nectar as 'good old corn' needed some disguise beyond seltzer.

'Say, boy,' exclaimed Clark breathlessly, 'doesn't Nancy Lamar look beautiful?'

Jim nodded.

'Mighty beautiful,' he agreed.

'She's all dolled up to a fare-you-well to-night,' continued Clark. 'Notice that fellow she's with?'

'Big fella? White pants?'

'Yeah. Well, that's Ogden Merritt from Savannah. Old man Merritt makes the Merritt safety razors. This fella's crazy about her. Been chasing after her all year.'

'She's a wild baby,' continued Clark, 'but I like her. So does everybody. But she sure does do crazy stunts. She usually gets out alive, but she's got scars all over her reputation from one thing or another she's done.'

'That so?' Jim passed over his glass. 'That's good corn.'

'Not so bad. Oh, she's a wild one. Shoots craps, say boy! And she do like her high-balls. Promised I'd give her one later on.'

'She in love with this—Merritt?'

'Damned if I know. Seems like all the best girls around here marry fellas and go off somewhere.'

He poured himself one more drink and carefully corked the bottle.

'Listen, Jim, I got to go dance and I'd be much obliged if you just stick this corn right on your hip as long as you're not dancing. If a man notices I've had a drink he'll come up and ask me and before I know it it's all gone and somebody else is having my good time.'

So Nancy Lamar was going to marry. This toast of a town was to become the private property of an individual in white trousers —and all because white trousers' father had made a better razor than his neighbour. As they descended the stairs Jim found the idea inexplicably depressing. For the first time in his life he felt a vague and romantic yearning. A picture of her began to form in his imagination—Nancy walking boy-like and debonnaire along the street, taking an orange as tithe from a worshipful fruit dealer, charging a dope on a mythical account at Soda Sam's, assembling a convoy of beaux and then driving off in triumphal state for an afternoon of splashing and singing.

The Jelly-bean walked out on the porch to a deserted corner, dark between the moon on the lawn and the single lighted door of the ballroom. There he found a chair and, lighting a cigarette, drifted into the thoughtless reverie that was his usual mood. Yet now it was a reverie made sensuous by the night and by the hot smell of damp powder puffs, tucked into the fronts of low dresses and distilling a thousand rich scents to float out through the open door. The music itself, blurred by a loud trombone, became hot and shadowy, a languorous overtone to the scraping of many shoes and slippers.

Suddenly the square of yellow light that fell through the door was obscured by a dark figure. A girl had come out of the dressing-room and was standing on the porch not more than ten feet away. Jim heard a low-breathed 'doggone' and then she turned and saw him. It was Nancy Lamar.

Jim rose to his feet.

'Howdy?'

'Hello—' She paused, hesitated and then approached. 'Oh, it's—Jim Powell.'

He bowed slightly, tried to think of a casual remark.

'Do you suppose,' she began quickly, 'I mean—do you know anything about gum?'

'What?'

'I've got gum on my shoe. Some utter ass left his or her gum on the floor and of course I stepped in it.'

Jim blushed, inappropriately.

'Do you know how to get it off?' she demanded petulantly. 'I've tried a knife. I've tried every damn thing in the dressing-room. I've tried soap and water—and even perfume and I've ruined my powder-puff trying to make it stick to that.'

Jim considered the question in some agitation.

'Why—I think maybe gasoline—'

The words had scarcely left his lips when she grasped his hand and pulled him at a run off the low veranda, over a flower bed and at a gallop towards a group of cars parked in the moonlight by the first hole of the golf course.

'Turn on the gasoline,' she commanded breathlessly.

'What?'

'For the gum of course. I've got to get it off. I can't dance with gum on.'

Obediently Jim turned to the cars and began inspecting them with a view to obtaining the desired solvent. Had she demanded a cylinder he would have done his best to wrench one out.

'Here,' he said after a moment's search. 'Here's one that's easy. Got a handkerchief?'

'It's up-stairs wet. I used it for the soap and water.'

Jim laboriously explored his pockets.

'Don't believe I've got one either.'

'Doggone it! Well, we can turn it on and let it run on the ground.'

He turned the spout; a dripping began.

'More!'

He turned it on fuller. The dripping became a flow and formed an oily pool that glistened brightly, reflecting a dozen tremulous moons on its quivering bosom.

'Ah,' she sighed contentedly, 'let it all out. The only thing to do is to wade in it.'

In desperation he turned on the tap full and the pool suddenly widened sending tiny rivers and trickles in all directions.

'That's fine. That's something like.'

Raising her skirts she stepped gracefully in.

'I know this'll take it off,' she murmured.

Jim smiled.

'There's lots more cars.'

She stepped daintily out of the gasoline and began scraping her slippers, side and bottom, on the running-board of the automobile. The Jelly-bean contained himself no longer. He bent double with explosive laughter and after a second she joined in.

'You're here with Clark Darrow, aren't you?' she asked as they walked back towards the veranda.

'Yes.'

'You know where he is now?'

'Out dancin', I reckon.'

'The deuce. He promised me a highball.'

'Well,' said Jim, 'I guess that'll be all right. I got his bottle right here in my pocket.'

She smiled at him radiantly.

'I guess maybe you'll need ginger ale though,' he added.

'Not me. Just the bottle.'

'Sure enough?'

She laughed scornfully.

'Try me. I can drink anything any man can. Let's sit down.'

She perched herself on the side of a table and he dropped into one of the wicker chairs beside her. Taking out the cork she held the flask to her lips and took a long drink. He watched her fascinated.

'Like it?'

She shook her head breathlessly.

'No, but I like the way it makes me feel. I think most people are that way.'

Jim agreed.

'My daddy liked it too well. It got him.'

'American men,' said Nancy gravely, 'don't know how to drink.'

'What?' Jim was startled.

'In fact,' she went on carelessly, 'they don't know how to do anything very well. The one thing I regret in my life is that I wasn't born in England.'

'In England?'

'Yes. It's the one regret of my life that I wasn't.'

'Do you like it over there?'

'Yes. Immensely. I've never been there in person, but I've met a lot of Englishmen who were over here in the army, Oxford and Cambridge men—you know, that's like Sewanee and University of Georgia are here—and of course I've read a lot of English novels.'

Jim was interested, amazed.

'D'you ever hear of Lady Diana Manners*?' she asked earnestly.

No, Jim had not.

'Well, she's what I'd like to be. Dark, you know, like me, and wild as sin. She's the girl who rode her horse up the steps of some cathedral or church or something and all the novelists made their heroines do it afterwards.'

Jim nodded politely. He was out of his depths.

'Pass the bottle,' suggested Nancy. 'I'm going to take another little one. A little drink wouldn't hurt a baby.'

'You see,' she continued, again breathless after a draught.

* An English actress, daughter of the Eighth Duke of Rutland and married to Alfred Duff Cooper, a senior politician.

'People over there have style. Nobody has style here. I mean the boys here aren't really worth dressing up for or doing sensational things for. Don't you know?'

'I suppose so—I mean I suppose not,' murmured Jim.

'And I'd like to do 'em an' all. I'm really the only girl in town that has style.'

She stretched out her arms and yawned pleasantly.

'Pretty evening.'

'Sure is,' agreed Jim.

'Like to have boat,' she suggested dreamily. 'Like to sail out on a silver lake, say the Thames for instance. Have champagne and caviare sandwiches along. Have about eight people. And one of the men would jump overboard to amuse the party and get drowned like a man did with Lady Diana Manners once.'

'Did he do it to please her?'

'Didn't mean drown himself to please her. He just meant to jump overboard and make everybody laugh.'

'I reckin they just died laughin' when he drowned.'

'Oh, I suppose they laughed a little,' she admitted. 'I imagine she did, anyway. She's pretty hard, I guess—like I am.'

'You hard?'

'Like nails.' She yawned again and added, 'Give me a little more from that bottle.'

Jim hesitated but she held out her hand defiantly.

'Don't treat me like a girl,' she warned him. 'I'm not like any girl *you* ever saw.' She considered. 'Still, perhaps you're right. You got—you got old head on young shoulders.'

She jumped to her feet and moved towards the door. The Jelly-bean rose also.

'Good-bye,' she said politely, 'good-bye. Thanks, Jelly-bean.'

Then she stepped inside and left him wide-eyed upon the porch.

III

At twelve o'clock a procession of cloaks issued single file from the women's dressing-room and, each one pairing with a coated beau like dancers meeting in a cotillion figure, drifted through the door with sleepy happy laughter—through the door into the dark where autos backed and snorted and parties called to one another and gathered around the water-cooler.

Jim, sitting in his corner, rose to look for Clark. They had met at eleven; then Clark had gone in to dance. So, seeking him, Jim wandered into the soft-drink stand that had once been a bar. The room was deserted except for a sleepy Negro dozing behind the counter and two boys lazily fingering a pair of dice at one of the tables. Jim was about to leave when he saw Clark coming in. At the same moment Clark looked up.

'Hi, Jim!' he commanded. 'C'mon over, and help us with this bottle. I guess there's not much left, but there's one all around.'

Nancy, the man from Savannah, Marylyn Wade, and Joe Ewing were lolling and laughing in the doorway. Nancy caught Jim's eye and winked at him humorously.

They drifted over to a table and arranging themselves around it waited for the waiter to bring ginger ale. Jim, faintly ill at ease, turned his eyes on Nancy, who had drifted into a nickel crap game with the two boys at the next table.

'Bring them over here,' suggested Clark.

Joe looked around.

'We don't want to draw a crowd. It's against club rules.'

'Nobody's around,' insisted Clark, 'except Mr Taylor. He's walking up and down like a wild man trying to find out who let all the gasoline out of his car.'

There was a general laugh.

'I bet a million Nancy got something on her shoe again. You can't park when she's around.'

'O Nancy, Mr Taylor's looking for you!'

Nancy's cheeks were glowing with excitement over the game. 'I haven't seen his silly little flivver* in two weeks.'

Jim felt a sudden silence. He turned and saw an individual of uncertain age standing in the doorway.

Clark's voice punctuated the embarrassment.

'Won't you join us, Mr Taylor?'

'Thanks.'

Mr Taylor spread his unwelcome presence over a chair. 'Have

---

*American slang term for a cheap, old, motor car.

to, I guess. I'm waiting till they dig me up some gasoline. Somebody got funny with my car.'

His eyes narrowed and he looked quickly from one to the other. Jim wondered what he had heard from the doorway—tried to remember what had been said.

'I'm right to-night,' Nancy sang out, 'and my four bits is in the ring.'

'Faded!' snapped Taylor suddenly.

'Why, Mr Taylor, I didn't know you shot craps!' Nancy was overjoyed to find that he had seated himself and instantly covered her bet. They had openly disliked each other since the night she had definitely discouraged a series of rather pointed advances.

'All right, babies, do it for your mamma. Just one little seven.' Nancy was *cooing* to the dice. She rattled them with a brave underhand flourish, and rolled them out on the table.

'Ah-h! I suspected it. And now again with the dollar up.'

Five passes to her credit found Taylor a bad loser. She was making it personal, and after each success Jim watched triumph flutter across her face. She was doubling with each throw—such luck could scarcely last.

'Better go easy,' he cautioned her timidly.

'Ah, but watch this one,' she whispered. It was eight on the dice and she called her number.

'Little Ada, this time we're going South.'

Ada from Decatur rolled over the table. Nancy was flushed and half-hysterical, but her luck was holding. She drove the pot up and up, refusing to drag. Taylor was drumming with his fingers on the table, but he was in to stay.

Then Nancy tried for a ten and lost the dice. Taylor seized them avidly. He shot in silence, and in the hush of excitement the clatter of one pass after another on the table was the only sound.

Now Nancy had the dice again, but her luck had broken. An hour passed. Back and forth it went. Taylor had been at it again —and again and again. They were even at last—Nancy lost her ultimate five dollars.

'Will you take my cheque,' she said quickly, 'for fifty, and we'll shoot it all?' Her voice was a little unsteady and her hand shook as she reached to the money.

Clark exchanged an uncertain but alarmed glance with Joe Ewing. Taylor shot again. He had Nancy's cheque.

'How 'bout another?' she said wildly. 'Jes' any bank'll do—money everywhere as a matter of fact.'

Jim understood—the 'good old corn' he had given her—the 'good old corn' she had taken since. He wished he dared interfere—a girl of that age and position would hardly have two bank accounts. When the clock struck two he contained himself no longer.

'May I—can't you let me roll 'em for you?' he suggested, his low, lazy voice a little strained.

Suddenly sleepy and listless, Nancy flung the dice down before him.

'All right—old boy! As Lady Diana Manners says, "Shoot 'em, Jelly-bean"—My luck's gone.'

'Mr Taylor,' said Jim, carelessly, 'we'll shoot for one of those there cheques against the cash.'

Half an hour later Nancy swayed forward and clapped him on the back.

'Stole my luck, you did.' She was nodding her head sagely.

Jim swept up the last cheque and putting it with the others tore them into confetti and scattered them on the floor. Someone started singing, and Nancy kicking her chair backwards rose to her feet.

'Ladies and gentlemen,' she announced. 'Ladies—that's you Marylyn. I want to tell the world that Mr Jim Powell, who is a well-known Jelly-bean of this city, is an exception to a great rule —"lucky in dice—unlucky in love". He's lucky in dice, and as matter fact I—I *love* him. Ladies and gentlemen, Nancy Lamar, famous dark-haired beauty often featured in the *Herald* as one th' most popular members of younger set as other girls are often featured in this particular case. Wish to announce—wish to announce, anyway, Gentlemen—' She tipped suddenly. Clark caught her and restored her balance.

'My error,' she laughed, 'she stoops to—stoops to—anyways—We'll drink to Jelly-bean . . . Mr Jim Powell, King of the Jelly-beans.'

And a few minutes later as Jim waited hat in hand for Clark in the darkness of that same corner of the porch where she had come searching for gasoline, she appeared suddenly beside him.

'Jelly-bean,' she said, 'are you here, Jelly-bean? I think—' and her slight unsteadiness seemed part of an enchanted dream— 'I think you deserve one of my sweetest kisses for that, Jelly-bean.'

For an instant her arms were around his neck—her lips were pressed to his.

'I'm a wild part of the world, Jelly-bean, but you did me a good turn.'

Then she was gone, down the porch, over the cricket-loud lawn. Jim saw Merritt come out the front door and say something to her angrily—saw her laugh and, turning away, walk with averted eyes to his car. Marylyn and Joe followed, singing a drowsy song, about a Jazz baby.

Clark came out and joined Jim on the steps. 'All pretty lit, I guess,' he yawned. 'Merritt's in a mean mood. He's certainly off Nancy.'

Over east along the golf course a faint rug of grey spread itself across the feet of the night. The party in the car began to chant a chorus as the engine warmed up.

'Good-night everybody,' called Clark.

'Good-night, Clark.'

'Good-night.'

There was a pause, and then a soft, happy voice added,

'Good-night, Jelly-bean.'

The car drove off to a burst of singing. A rooster on a farm across the way took up a solitary mournful crow, and behind them a last Negro waiter turned out the porch light. Jim and Clark strolled over towards the Ford, their shoes crunching raucously on the gravel drive.

'Oh boy!' sighed Clark softly, 'how you can set those dice!'

It was still too dark for him to see the flush on Jim's thin cheeks—or to know that it was a flush of unfamiliar shame.

IV

Over Tilly's garage a bleak room echoed all day to the rumble and snorting down-stairs and the singing of the Negro washers as they turned the hose on the cars outside. It was a cheerless square of a room, punctuated with a bed and a battered table on which lay half a dozen books—Joe Miller's 'Slow Train thru Arkansas', 'Lucille', in an old edition very much annotated in an old-fashioned hand; 'The Eyes of the World', by Harold Bell Wright, and an ancient prayer-book of the Church of England with the name Alice Powell and the date 1831 written on the fly-leaf.

The East, grey when the Jelly-bean entered the garage, became a rich and vivid blue as he turned on his solitary electric light. He snapped it out again, and going to the window rested his elbows on the sill and stared into the deepening morning. With the awakening of his emotions, his first perception was a sense of futility, a dull ache at the utter greyness of his life. A wall had sprung up suddenly around him hedging him in, a wall as definite and tangible as the white wall of his bare room. And with his perception of this wall all that had been the romance of his existence, the casualness, the light-hearted improvidence, the miraculous open-handedness of life, faded out. The Jelly-bean strolling up Jackson Street humming a lazy song, known at every shop and street stand, cropful of easy greeting and local wit, sad sometimes for only the sake of sadness and the flight of time —that Jelly-bean was suddenly vanished. The very name was a reproach, a triviality. With a flood of insight he knew that Merritt must despise him, that even Nancy's kiss in the dawn would have awakened not jealousy but only a contempt for Nancy's so lowering herself. And on his part the Jelly-bean had used for her a dingy subterfuge learned from the garage. He had been her moral laundry; the stains were his.

As the grey became blue, brightened and filled the room, he crossed to his bed and threw himself down on it, gripping the edges fiercely.

'I love her,' he cried aloud, 'God!'

As he said this something gave way within him like a lump melting in his throat. The air cleared and became radiant with dawn, and turning over on his face he began to sob dully into the pillow.

In the sunshine of three o'clock Clark Darrow chugging painfully along Jackson Street was hailed by the Jelly-bean, who stood on the curb with his fingers in his vest pockets.

'Hi!' called Clark, bringing his Ford to an astonishing stop alongside. 'Just get up?'

The Jelly-bean shook his head.

'Never did go to bed. Felt sorta restless, so I took a long walk this morning out in the country. Just got into town this minute.'

'Should think you *would* feel restless. I been feeling thataway all day—'

'I'm thinkin' of leavin' town,' continued the Jelly-bean, absorbed by his own thoughts. 'Been thinkin' of goin' up on the farm, and takin' a little that work off Uncle Dun. Reckin I been bummin' too long.'

Clark was silent and the Jelly-bean continued:

'I reckin maybe after Aunt Mamie dies I could sink that money of mine in the farm and make somethin' out of it. All my people originally came from that part up there. Had a big place.'

Clark looked at him curiously.

'That's funny,' he said. 'This—this sort of affected me the same way.'

The Jelly-bean hesitated.

'I don't know,' he began slowly, 'somethin' about—about that girl last night talkin' about a lady named Diana Manners—an English lady, sorta got me thinkin'!' He drew himself up and looked oddly at Clark, 'I had a family once,' he said defiantly.

Clark nodded.

'I know.'

'And I'm the last of 'em,' continued the Jelly-bean, his voice rising slightly, 'and I ain't worth shucks. Name they call me by means jelly—weak and wobbly like. People who weren't nothin' when my folks was a lot turn up their noses when they pass me on the street.'

Again Clark was silent.

'So I'm through. I'm goin' to-day. And when I come back to this town it's going to be like a gentleman.'

Clark took out his handkerchief and wiped his damp brow.

'Reckon you're not the only one it shook up,' he admitted gloomily. 'All this thing of girls going round like they do is going to stop right quick. Too bad, too, but everybody'll have to see it thataway.

'Do you mean,' demanded Jim in surprise, 'that all that's leaked out?'

'Leaked out? How on earth could they keep it secret. It'll be announced in the papers to-night. Doctor Lamar's got to save his name somehow.'

Jim put his hands on the sides of the car and tightened his long fingers on the metal.

'Do you mean Taylor investigated those cheques?'

It was Clark's turn to be surprised.

'Haven't you heard what happened?'

Jim's startled eyes were answer enough.

'Why,' announced Clark dramatically, 'those four got another bottle of corn, got tight and decided to shock the town—so Nancy and that fella Merritt were married in Rockville at seven o'clock this morning.'

A tiny indentation appeared in the metal under the Jelly-bean's fingers.

'Married?'

'Sure enough. Nancy sobered up and rushed back into town, crying and frightened to death—claimed it'd all been a mistake. First Doctor Lamar went wild and was going to kill Merritt, but finally they got it patched up some way, and Nancy and Merritt went to Savannah on the two-thirty train.'

Jim closed his eyes and with an effort overcame a sudden sickness.

'It's too bad,' said Clark philosophically. 'I don't mean the wedding—reckon that's all right, though I don't guess Nancy cared a darn about him. But it's a crime for a nice girl like that to hurt her family that way.'

The Jelly-bean let go the car and turned away. Again something was going on inside him, some inexplicable but almost chemical change.

'Where you going?' asked Clark.

The Jelly-bean turned and looked dully back over his shoulder.

'Got to go,' he muttered. 'Been up too long; feelin' right sick.'

'Oh.'

The street was hot at three and hotter still at four, the April dust seeming to enmesh the sun and give it forth again as a world-old joke forever played on an eternity of afternoons. But at half-past four a first layer of quiet fell and the shades lengthened under the awnings and heavy foliaged trees. In this heat nothing mattered. All life was weather, a waiting through the hot where events had no significance for the cool that was soft and caressing like a woman's hand on a tired forehead. Down in Georgia there is a feeling—perhaps inarticulate—that this is the greatest wisdom of the South—so after a while the Jelly-bean turned into a pool-hall on Jackson Street where he was sure to find a congenial crowd who would make all the old jokes—the ones he knew.

Outside the Cabinet-Maker's

The automobile stopped at the corner of Sixteenth and some dingy-looking street. The lady got out. The man and the little girl stayed in the car.

'I'm going to tell him it can't cost more than twenty dollars,' said the lady.

'All right. Have you the plans?'

'Oh, yes'—she reached for her bag in the back seat—'at least I have now.'

'Dites qu'il ne faut pas avoir des forts placards,' said the man. 'Ni du bon bois.'

'All right.'

'I wish you wouldn't talk French,' said the little girl.

'Et il faut avoir un bon "height". L'un des Murphys était comme ça.'

He held his hand five feet from the ground. The lady went through a door lettered 'Cabinet-Maker' and disappeared up a small stairs.

The man and the little girl looked around unexpectantly. The neighbourhood was red brick, vague, quiet. There were a few darkies doing something or other up the street and an occasional automobile went by. It was a fine November day.

'Listen,' said the man to the little girl. 'I love you.'

'I love you too,' said the little girl, smiling politely.

'Listen,' the man continued. 'Do you see that house over the way?'

The little girl looked. It was a flat in back of a shop. Curtains masked most of its interior, but there was a faint stir behind them. On one window a loose shutter banged from back to forth every few minutes. Neither the man nor the little girl had ever seen the place before.

'There's a Fairy Princess behind those curtains,' said the man. 'You can't see her but she's there, kept concealed by an Ogre. Do you know what an Ogre is?'

'Yes.'

'Well, this Princess is very beautiful with long golden hair.'

They both regarded the house. Part of a yellow dress appeared momentarily in the window.

'That's her,' the man said. 'The people who live there are guarding her for the Ogre. He's keeping the King and Queen prisoner ten thousand miles below the earth. She can't get out until the Prince finds the three—' He hesitated.

'And what, Daddy? The three what?'

'The three—Look! There she is again.'

'The three what?'

'The three—the three stones that will release the King and Queen.'

He yawned.

'And what then?'

'Then he can come and tap three times on each window and that will set her free.'

The lady's head emerged from the upper storey of the cabinet-maker's.

'He's busy,' she called down. 'Gosh, what a nice day!'

'And what, Daddy?' asked the little girl. 'Why does the Ogre want to keep her there?'

'Because he wasn't invited to the christening. The Prince has already found one stone in President Coolidge's collarbox. He's looking for the second in Iceland. Every time he finds a stone the room where the Princess is kept turns blue. *Gosh!*'

'What, Daddy?'

'Just as you turned away I could see the room turn blue. That means he's found the second stone.'

'Gosh!' said the little girl. 'Look! It turned blue again. That means he's found the third stone.'

Aroused by the competition the man looked around cautiously and his voice grew tense.

'Do you see what I see?' he demanded. 'Coming up the street —there's the Ogre himself, disguised—you know: transformed, like Mombi in *The Land of Oz.*'

'I know.'

They both watched. The small boy, extraordinarily small and taking very long steps, went to the door of the flat and knocked; no one answered, but he didn't seem to expect it or to be greatly disappointed. He took some chalk from his pocket and began drawing pictures under the doorbell.

'He's making magic signs,' whispered the man. 'He wants to be sure that the Princess doesn't get out this door. He must know that the Prince has set the King and Queen free and will be along for her pretty soon.'

The small boy lingered for a moment; then he went to a window and called an unintelligible word. After a while a woman threw the window open and made an answer that the crisp wind blew away.

'She says she's got the Princess locked up,' explained the man.

'Look at the Ogre,' said the little girl. 'He's making magic signs under the window too. And on the sidewalk. Why?'

'He wants to keep her from getting out, of course. That's why he's dancing. That's a charm too—it's a magic dance.'

The Ogre went away, taking very big steps. Two men crossed the street ahead and passed out of sight.

'Who are they, Daddy?'

'They're two of the King's soldiers. I think the army must be gathering over on Market Street to surround the house. Do you know what "surround" means?'

'Yes. Are those men soldiers too?'

'Those too. And I believe that the old one just behind is the King himself. He's keeping bent down low like that so that the Ogre's people won't recognize him.'

'Who is the lady?'

'She's a Witch, a friend of the Ogre's.'

The shutter blew closed with a bang and then slowly opened again.

'That's done by the good and bad fairies,' the man explained. 'They're invisible, but the bad fairies want to close the shutter so nobody can see in and the good ones want to open it.'

'The good fairies are winning now.'

'Yes.' He looked at the little girl. 'You're my good fairy.'

'Yes. Look, Daddy! What is that man?'

'He's in the King's army too.' The clerk of Mr Miller, the jeweller, went by with a somewhat unmartial aspect. 'Hear the whistle? That means they're gathering. And listen—there goes the drum.'

'There's the Queen, Daddy. Look at there. Is that the Queen?'

'No, that's a girl called Miss Television.' He yawned. He began to think of something pleasant that had happened yesterday. He went into a trance. Then he looked at the little girl and saw that she was quite happy. She was six and lovely to look at. He kissed her.

'That man carrying the cake of ice is also one of the King's soldiers,' he said. 'He's going to put the ice on the Ogre's head and freeze his brains so he can't do any more harm.'

Her eyes followed the man down street. Other men passed. A darky in a yellow darky's overcoat drove by with a cart marked The Del Upholstery Co. The shutter banged again and then slowly opened.

'See, Daddy, the good fairies are winning again.'

The man was old enough to know that he would look back to that time—the tranquil street and the pleasant weather and the mystery playing before the child's eyes, mystery which he had created, but whose lustre and texture he could never see or touch any more himself. Again, he touched his daughter's cheek instead and in payment fitted another small boy and limping man into the story.

'Oh, I love you,' he said.

'I know, Daddy,' she answered, abstractedly. She was staring at the house. For a moment he closed his eyes and tried to see with her but he couldn't see—those ragged blinds were drawn against him forever. There were only the occasional darkies and the small boys and the weather that reminded him of more glamorous mornings in the past.

The lady came out of the cabinet-maker's shop.

'How did it go?' he asked.

'Good. Il dit qu'il a fait les maisons de poupée pour les Du Ponts. Il va le faire.'

'Combien?'

'Vingt-cinq. I'm sorry I was so long.'

'Look, Daddy, there go a lot more soldiers!'

They drove off. When they had gone a few miles the man turned around and said, 'We saw the most remarkable thing while you were there.' He summarized the episode. 'It's too bad we couldn't wait and see the rescue.'

'But we did,' the child cried. 'They had the rescue in the next street. And there's the Ogre's body in that yard there. The King and Queen and Prince were killed and now the Princess is queen.'

He had liked his King and Queen and felt that they had been too summarily disposed of.

'You had to have a heroine,' he said rather impatiently.

'She'll marry someone and make him Prince.'

They rode on abstractedly. The lady thought about the doll's house, for she had been poor and had never had one as a child, the man thought about how he had almost a million dollars, and the little girl thought about the odd doings on the dingy street that they had left behind.

What a Handsome Pair!

At four o'clock on a November afternoon in 1902, Teddy Van Beck got out of a hansom cab in front of a brownstone house on Murray Hill. He was a tall, round-shouldered young man with a beaked nose and soft brown eyes in a sensitive face. In his veins quarrelled the blood of colonial governors and celebrated robber barons; in him the synthesis had produced, for that time and place, something different and something new.

His cousin, Helen Van Beck, waited in the drawing-room.

Her eyes were red from weeping, but she was young enough for it not to detract from her glossy beauty—a beauty that had reached the point where it seemed to contain in itself the secret of its own growth, as if it would go on increasing forever. She was nineteen and, contrary to the evidence, she was extremely happy.

Teddy put his arm around her and kissed her cheek, and found it changing into her ear as she turned her face away. He held her for a moment, his own enthusiasm chilling; then he said:

'You don't seem very glad to see me.'

Helen had a premonition that this was going to be one of the most memorable scenes of her life, and with unconscious cruelty she set about extracting from it its full dramatic value. She sat in a corner of the couch, facing an easy-chair.

'Sit there,' she commanded, in what was then admired as a 'regal manner', and then, as Teddy straddled the piano stool: 'No, don't sit there. I can't talk to you if you're going to revolve around.'

'Sit on my lap,' he suggested.

'No.'

Playing a one-handed flourish on the piano, he said, 'I can listen better here.'

Helen gave up hopes of beginning on the sad and quiet note.

'This is a serious matter, Teddy. Don't think I've decided it without a lot of consideration. I've got to ask you—to ask you to release me from our understanding.'

'What?' Teddy's face paled with shock and dismay.

'I'll have to tell you from the beginning. I've realised for a long time that we have nothing in common. You're interested in your music, and I can't even play chopsticks.' Her voice was weary as if with suffering; her small teeth tugged at her lower lip.

'What of it?' he demanded, relieved. 'I'm musician enough for both. You wouldn't have to understand banking to marry a banker, would you?'

'This is different,' Helen answered. 'What would we do together? One important thing is that you don't like riding; you told me you were afraid of horses.'

'Of course I'm afraid of horses,' he said, and added reminiscently: 'They try to bite me.'

'It makes it so—'

'I've never met a horse—socially, that is—who didn't try to bite me. They used to do it when I put the bridle on; then, when I gave up putting the bridle on, they began reaching their heads around trying to get at my calves.'

The eyes of her father, who had given her a Shetland at three, glistened, cold and hard, from her own.

'You don't even like the people I like, let alone the horses,' she said.

'I can stand them. I've stood them all my life.'

'Well, it would be a silly way to start a marriage. I don't see any grounds for mutual—mutual—'

'Riding?'

'Oh, not that.' Helen hesitated, and then said in an unconvinced tone, 'Probably I'm not clever enough for you.'

'Don't talk such stuff!' He demanded some truth: 'Who's the man?'

It took her a moment to collect herself. She had always resented Teddy's tendency to treat women with less ceremony than was the custom of the day. Often he was an unfamiliar, almost frightening young man.

'There is someone,' she admitted. 'It's someone I've always known slightly, but about a month ago, when I went to Southampton, I was—thrown with him.'

'Thrown from a horse?'

'Please, Teddy,' she protested gravely. 'I'd been getting more unhappy about you and me, and whenever I was with him everything seemed all right.' A note of exaltation that she would not conceal came into Helen's voice. She rose and crossed the room, her straight, slim legs outlined by the shadows of her dress. 'We rode and swam and played tennis together—did the things we both liked to do.'

He stared into the vacant space she had created for him. 'Is that all that drew you to this fellow?'

'No, it was more than that. He was thrilling to me like nobody has ever been.' She laughed, 'I think what really started me thinking about it was one day we came in from riding and everybody said aloud what a nice pair we made.'

'Did you kiss him?'

She hesitated. 'Yes, once.'

He got up from the piano stool. 'I feel as if I had a cannon ball in my stomach,' he exclaimed.

The butler announced Mr Stuart Oldhorne.

'Is he the man?' Teddy demanded tensely.

She was suddenly upset and confused. 'He should have come later. Would you rather go without meeting him?'

But Stuart Oldhorne, made confident by his new sense of proprietorship, had followed the butler.

The two men regarded each other with a curious impotence of expression; there can be no communication between men in that position, for their relation is indirect and consists in how much each of them has possessed or will possess of the woman in question, so that their emotions pass through her divided self as through a bad telephone connection.

Stuart Oldhorne sat beside Helen, his polite eyes never leaving Teddy. He had the same glowing physical power as she. He had been a star athlete at Yale and a Rough Rider in Cuba, and was the best young horseman on Long Island. Women loved him not only for his points but for a real sweetness of temper.

'You've lived so much in Europe that I don't often see you,' he said to Teddy. Teddy didn't answer and Stuart Oldhorne turned to Helen. 'I'm early; I didn't realise—'

'You came at the right time,' said Teddy rather harshly. 'I stayed to play you my congratulations.'

To Helen's alarm, he turned and ran his fingers over the keyboard. Then he began.

What he was playing, neither Helen nor Stuart knew, but Teddy always remembered. He put his mind in order with a short résumé of the history of music, beginning with some chords from The Messiah and ending with Debussy's La Plus Que Lent, which had an evocative quality for him, because he had first heard it the day his brother died. Then, pausing for an instant, he began to play more thoughtfully, and the lovers on the sofa could feel that they were alone—that he had left them and had no more traffic with them—and Helen's discomfort lessened. But the flight, the elusiveness of the music, piqued her, gave her a feeling of annoyance. If Teddy had played the current sentimental song from Erminie, and had played it with feeling, she would have understood and been moved, but he was plunging her suddenly into a world of mature emotions, whither her nature neither could nor wished to follow.

She shook herself slightly and said to Stuart: 'Did you buy the horse?'

'Yes, and at a bargain . . . Do you know I love you?'

'I'm glad,' she whispered.

The piano stopped suddenly. Teddy closed it and swung slowly around: 'Did you like my congratulations?'

'Very much,' they said together.

'It was pretty good,' he admitted. 'That last was only based on a little counterpoint. You see, the idea of it was that you make such a handsome pair.'

He laughed unnaturally; Helen followed him out into the hall.

'Good-bye, Teddy,' she said. 'We're going to be good friends, aren't we?'

'Aren't we?' he repeated. He winked without smiling, and with a clicking, despairing sound of his mouth, went out quickly.

For a moment Helen tried vainly to apply a measure to the situation, wondering how she had come off with him, realising reluctantly that she had never for an instant held the situation in her hands. She had a dim realisation that Teddy was larger in scale; then the very largeness frightened her and, with relief and a warm tide of emotion, she hurried into the drawing-room and the shelter of her lover's arms.

Their engagement ran through a halcyon summer, Stuart visited Helen's family at Tuxedo, and Helen visited his family in Wheatley Hills. Before breakfast, their horses' hoofs sedately scattered the dew in sentimental glades, or curtained them with dust as they raced on dirt roads. They bought a tandem bicycle and pedalled all over Long Island—which Mrs Cassius Ruthven, a contemporary Cato,* considered 'rather fast' for a couple not yet married.

Helen's taste for sport was advanced for her generation. She rode nearly as well as Stuart and gave him a decent game in tennis. He taught her some polo, and they were golf crazy when it was still considered a comic game. They liked to feel fit and

*Cato: a conservative and moral statesman, 234-149 B.C., who attempted to preserve Rome from Greek influence.

cool together. They thought of themselves as a team, and it was often remarked how well mated they were. A chorus of pleasant envy followed in the wake of their effortless glamour.

They talked.

'It seems a pity you've got to go to the office,' she would say. 'I wish you did something we could do together, like taming lions.'

'I've always thought that in a pinch I could make a living breeding and racing horses,' said Stuart.

'I know you could, you darling.'

In August he brought a Thomas automobile and toured all the way to Chicago with three other men. It was an event of national interest and their pictures were in all the papers. Helen wanted to go, but it wouldn't have been proper, so they compromised by driving down Fifth Avenue on a sunny September morning, one with the fine day and the fashionable crowd, but distinguished by their unity, which made them each as strong as two.

'What do you suppose?' Helen demanded. 'Teddy sent me the oddest present—a cup rack.'

Stuart laughed. 'Obviously, he means that all we'll ever do is win cups.'

'I thought it was rather a slam,' Helen ruminated. 'I saw that he was invited to everything, but he didn't answer a single invitation. Would you mind very much stopping by his apartment now? I haven't seen him for months and I don't like to leave anything unpleasant in the past.'

He wouldn't go in with her. 'I'll sit and answer questions about the auto from passers-by.'

The door was opened by a woman in a cleaning cap, and Helen heard the sound of Teddy's piano from the room beyond. The woman seemed reluctant to admit her.

'He said don't interrupt him, but I suppose if you're his cousin—'

Teddy welcomed her, obviously startled and somewhat upset, but in a minute he was himself again.

'I won't marry you,' he assured her. 'You've had your chance.'

'All right,' she laughed.

'How are you?' He threw a pillow at her. 'You're beautiful! Are you happy with this—this centaur? Does he beat you with his riding crop?' He peered at her closely. 'You look a little duller than when I knew you. I used to whip you up to a nervous excitement that bore a resemblance to intelligence.'

'I'm happy, Teddy. I hope you are.'

'Sure, I'm happy; I'm working. I've got MacDowell on the run and I'm going to have a shebang at Carnegie Hall next September.' His eyes became malicious. 'What did you think of my girl?'

'Your girl?'

'The girl who opened the door for you.'

'Oh, I thought it was a maid.' She flushed and was silent.

He laughed. 'Hey, Betty!' he called. 'You were mistaken for the maid!'

'And that's the fault of my cleaning on Sunday,' answered a voice from the next room.

Teddy lowered his voice. 'Do you like her?' he demanded.

'Teddy!' She teetered on the arm of the sofa, wondering whether she should leave at once.

'What would you think if I married her?' he asked confidentially.

'Teddy!' She was outraged; it had needed but a glance to place the woman as common. 'You're joking. She's older than you . . . You wouldn't be such a fool as to throw away your future that way.'

He didn't answer.

'Is she musical?' Helen demanded. 'Does she help you with your work?'

'She doesn't know a note. Neither did you, but I've got enough music in me for twenty wives.'

Visualising herself as one of them, Helen rose stiffly.

'All I can ask you is to think how your mother would have felt —and those who care for you . . . Good-bye, Teddy.'

He walked out the door with her and down the stairs.

'As a matter of fact, we've been married for two months,' he said casually. 'She was a waitress in a place where I used to eat.'

Helen felt that she should be angry and aloof, but tears of hurt vanity were springing to her eyes.

'And do you love her?'

'I like her; she's a good person and good for me. Love is something else. I loved you, Helen, and that's all dead in me for the present. Maybe it's coming out in my music. Some day I'll probably love other women—or maybe there'll never be anything but you. Good-bye, Helen.'

The declaration touched her. 'I hope you'll be happy, Teddy. Bring your wife to the wedding.'

He bowed noncommitally. When she had gone, he returned thoughtfully to his apartment.

'That was the cousin that I was in love with,' he said.

'And was it?' Betty's face, Irish and placid, brightened with interest. 'She's a pretty thing.'

'She wouldn't have been as good for me as a nice peasant like you.'

'Always thinking of yourself, Teddy Van Beck.'

He laughed. 'Sure I am, but you love me, anyhow?'

'That's a big wur-red.'

'All right. I'll remember that when you come begging around for a kiss. If my grandfather knew I married a bog trotter, he'd turn over in his grave. Now get out and let me finish my work.'

He sat at the piano, a pencil behind his ear. Already his face was resolved, composed, but his eyes grew more intense minute by minute, until there was a glaze in them, behind which they seemed to have joined his ears in counting and hearing. Presently there was no more indication in his face that anything had occurred to disturb the tranquillity of his Sunday morning.

II

Mrs Cassius Ruthven and a friend, veils flung back across their hats, sat in their auto on the edge of the field.

'A young woman playing polo in breeches.' Mrs Ruthven sighed. 'Amy Van Beck's daughter. I thought when Helen organised the Amazons she'd stop at divided skirts. But her husband apparently has no objections, for there he stands, egging her on. Of course, they always have liked the same things.'

'A pair of thoroughbreds, those two,' said the other woman complacently, meaning that she admitted them to be her equals. 'You'd never look at them and think that anything had gone wrong.'

She was referring to Stuart's mistake in the panic of 1907. His father had bequeathed him a precarious situation and Stuart had made an error of judgment. His honour was not questioned and his crowd stood by him loyally, but his usefulness in Wall Street was over and his small fortune was gone.

He stood in a group of men with whom he would presently play, noting things to tell Helen after the game—she wasn't turning with the play soon enough and several times she was unnecessarily ridden off at important moments. Her ponies were sluggish—the penalty for playing with borrowed mounts—but she was, nevertheless, the best player on the field, and in the last minute she made a save that brought applause.

'Good girl! Good girl!'

Stuart had been delegated with the unpleasant duty of chasing the women from the field. They had started an hour late and now a team from New Jersey was waiting to play; he sensed trouble as he cut across to join Helen and walked beside her toward the stables. She was splendid, with her flushed cheeks, her shining, triumphant eyes, her short, excited breath. He temporised for a minute.

'That was good—that last,' he said.

'Thanks. It almost broke my arm. Wasn't I pretty good all through?'

'You were the best out there.'

'I know it.'

He waited while she dismounted and handed the pony to a groom.

'Helen, I believe I've got a job.'

'What is it?'

'Don't jump on the idea till you think it over. Gus Myers wants me to manage his racing stables. Eight thousand a year.'

Helen considered. 'It's a nice salary; and I bet you could make yourself up a nice string from his ponies.'

'The principal thing is that I need the money; I'd have as much as you and things would be easier.'

'You'd have as much as me,' Helen repeated. She almost regretted that he would need no more help from her. 'But with Gus Myers, isn't there a string attached? Wouldn't he expect a boost up?'

'He probably would,' answered Stuart bluntly, 'and if I can help him socially, I will. As a matter of fact, he wants me at a stag dinner tonight.'

'All right, then,' Helen said absently. Still hesitating to tell her her game was over, Stuart followed her glance toward the field, where a runabout had driven up and parked by the ropes.

'There's your old friend, Teddy,' he remarked dryly—'or rather, your new friend, Teddy. He's taking a sudden interest in polo. Perhaps he thinks the horses aren't biting this summer.'

'You're not in very good humour,' protested Helen. 'You know, if you say the word, I'll never see him again. All I want in the world is for you and I to be together.'

'I know,' he admitted regretfully. 'Selling horses and giving up clubs put a crimp in that. I know the women all fall for Teddy, now he's getting famous, but if he tries to fool around with you I'll break his piano over his head . . . Oh, another thing,' he began, seeing the men already riding on the field. 'About your last chukker—'

As best he could, he put the situation up to her. He was not prepared for the fury that swept over her.

'But it's an outrage! I got up the game and it's been posted on the bulletin board for three days.'

'You started an hour late.'

'And do you know why?' she demanded. 'Because your friend Joe Morgan insisted that Celie ride sidesaddle. He tore her habit off her three times, and she only got here by climbing out the kitchen window.'

'I can't do anything about it.'

'Why can't you? Weren't you once a governor of this club? How can women expect to be any good if they have to quit every time the men want the field? All the men want is for the women to come up to them in the evening and tell them what a beautiful game they played!'

Still raging and blaming Stuart, she crossed the field to Teddy's car. He got out and greeted her with concentrated intensity:

'I've reached the point where I can neither sleep nor eat from thinking of you. What point is that?'

There was something thrilling about him that she had never been conscious of in the old days; perhaps the stories of his philanderings had made him more romantic to her.

'Well, don't think of me as I am now,' she said. 'My face is getting rougher every day and my muscles lean out of an evening dress like a female impersonator. People are beginning to refer to me as handsome instead of pretty. Besides, I'm in a vile humour. It seems to me women are always just edged out of everything.'

Stuart's game was brutal that afternoon. In the first five minutes, he realised that Teddy's runabout was no longer there, and his long slugs began to tally from all angles. Afterward, he bumped home across country at a gallop; his mood was not assuaged by a note handed by the children's nurse:

Dear: Since your friends made it impossible for us to play, I wasn't going to sit there just dripping; so I had Teddy bring me home. And since you'll be out to dinner, I'm going into New York with him to the theatre. I'll either be out on the theatre train or spend the night at mother's.

HELEN

Stuart went upstairs and changed into his dinner coat. He had no defence against the unfamiliar claws of jealousy that began a slow dissection of his insides. Often Helen had gone to plays or dances with other men, but this was different. He felt toward Teddy the faint contempt of the physical man for the artist, but the last six months had bruised his pride. He perceived the possibility that Helen might be seriously interested in someone else.

He was in a bad humour at Gus Myers' dinner—annoyed with his host for talking so freely about their business arrangement. When at last they rose from the table, he decided that it was no go and called Myers aside.

'Look here, I'm afraid this isn't a good idea, after all.'

'Why not?' His host looked at him in alarm. 'Are you going back on me? My dear fellow—'

'I think we'd better call it off.'

'And why, may I ask? Certainly I have the right to ask why.'

Stuart considered. 'All right, I'll tell you. When you made

that little speech, you mentioned me as if you had somehow
bought me, as if I was a sort of employee in your office. Now,
in the sporting world that doesn't go; things are more—more
democratic. I grew up with all these men here tonight, and they
didn't like it any better than I did.'

'I see,' Mr Myers reflected carefully—'I see.' Suddenly he
clapped Stuart on the back. 'That is exactly the sort of thing I
like to be told; it helps me. From now on I won't mention you
as if you were in my—as if we had a business arrangement. Is that
all right?'

After all, the salary was eight thousand dollars.

'Very well, then,' Stuart agreed. 'But you'll have to excuse
me tonight. I'm catching a train to the city.'

'I'll put an automobile at your disposal.'

At ten o'clock he rang the bell of Teddy's apartment on
Forty-eighth Street.

'I'm looking for Mr Van Beck,' he said to the woman who
answered the door. 'I know he's gone to the theatre, but I
wonder if you can tell me—' Suddenly he guessed who the
woman was. 'I'm Stuart Oldhorne,' he explained. 'I married Mr
Van Beck's cousin.'

'Oh, come in,' said Betty pleasantly. 'I know all about who
you are.'

She was just this side of forty, stoutish and plain of face, but
full of a keen, brisk vitality. In the living room they sat down.

'You want to see Teddy?'

'He's with my wife and I want to join them after the theatre. I
wonder if you know where they went?'

'Oh, so Teddy's with your wife.' There was a faint pleasant
brogue in her voice. 'Well, now, he didn't say exactly where
he'd be tonight.'

'Then you don't know?'

'I don't know—not for the life of me,' she admitted cheer-
fully. 'I'm sorry.'

He stood up, and Betty saw the thinly hidden anguish in his
face. Suddenly she was really sorry.

'I did hear him say something about the theatre,' she said
ruminatively. 'Now sit down and let me think what it was. He
goes out so much and a play once a week is enough for me, so

that one night mixes up with the others in my head. Didn't your wife say where to meet them?'

'No. I only decided to come in after they'd started. She said she'd catch the theatre train back to Long Island or go to her mother's.'

'That's it,' Betty said triumphantly, striking her hands together like cymbals. 'That's what he said when he called up—that he was putting a lady on the theatre train for Long Island, and would be home himself right afterward. We've had a child sick and it's driven things from my mind.'

'I'm very sorry I bothered you under those conditions.'

'It's no bother. Sit down. It's only just after ten.'

Feeling easier, Stuart relaxed a little and accepted a cigar.

'No, if I tried to keep up with Teddy, I'd have white hair by now,' Betty said. 'Of course, I go to his concerts, but often I fall asleep—not that he ever knows it. So long as he doesn't take too much to drink and knows where his home is, I don't bother about where he wanders.' As Stuart's face grew serious again, she changed her tone: 'All and all, he's a good husband to me and we have a happy life together, without interfering with each other. How would he do working next to the nursery and groaning at every sound? And how would I do going to Mrs Ruthven's with him, and all of them talking about high society and high art?'

A phrase of Helen's came back to Stuart: 'Always together—I like for us to do everything together.'

'You have children, haven't you, Mr Oldhorne?'

'Yes. My boy's almost big enough to sit a horse.'

'Ah, yes; you're both great for horses.'

'My wife says that as soon as their legs are long enough to reach stirrups, she'll be interested in them again.' This didn't sound right to Stuart and he modified it: 'I mean she always has been interested in them, but she never let them monopolise her or come between us. We've always believed that marriage ought to be founded on companionship, on having the same interests. I mean, you're musical and you help your husband.'

Betty laughed. 'I wish Teddy could hear that. I can't read a note or carry a tune.'

'No?' He was confused. 'I'd somehow got the impression that

you were musical.'

'You can't see why else he'd have married me?'

'Not at all. On the contrary.'

After a few minutes, he said good night, somehow liking her. When he had gone, Betty's expression changed slowly to one of exasperation; she went to the telephone and called her husband's studio:

'There you are, Teddy. Now listen to me carefully. I know your cousin is with you and I want to talk with her . . . Now, don't lie. You put her on the phone. Her husband has been here, and if you don't let me talk to her, it might be a serious matter.'

She could hear an unintelligible colloquy, and then Helen's voice:

'Hello.'

'Good evening, Mrs Oldhorne. Your husband came here, looking for you and Teddy. I told him I didn't know which play you were at, so you'd better be thinking which one. And I told him Teddy was leaving you at the station in time for the theatre train.'

'Oh, thank you very much. We—'

'Now, you meet your husband or there's trouble for you, or I'm no judge of men. And—wait a minute. Tell Teddy, if he's going to be up late, that Josie's sleeping light, and he's not to touch the piano when he gets home.'

Betty heard Teddy come in at eleven, and she came into the drawing-room smelling of camomile vapour. He greeted her absently; there was a look of suffering in his face and his eyes were bright and far away.

'You call yourself a great musician, Teddy Van Beck,' she said, 'but it seems to me you're much more interested in women.'

'Let me alone, Betty.'

'I do let you alone, but when the husbands start coming here, it's another matter.'

'This was different, Betty. This goes way back into the past.'

'It sounds like the present to me.'

'Don't make any mistake about Helen,' he said. 'She's a good woman.'

'Not through any fault of yours, I know.'

He sank his head wearily in his hands. 'I've tried to forget her. I've avoided her for six years. And then, when I met her a month ago, it all rushed over me. Try and understand, Bet. You're my best friend; you're the only person that ever loved me.'

'When you're good I love you,' she said.

'Don't worry. It's over. She loves her husband; she just came to New York with me because she's got some spite against him. She follows me a certain distance just like she always has, and then—Anyhow, I'm not going to see her any more. Now go to bed, Bet. I want to play for a while.'

He was on his feet when she stopped him.

'You're not to touch the piano tonight.'

'Oh, I forgot about Josie,' he said remorsefully. 'Well, I'll drink a bottle of beer and then I'll come to bed.'

He came close and put his arm around her.

'Dear Bet, nothing could ever interfere with us.'

'You're a bad boy, Teddy,' she said. 'I wouldn't ever be so bad to you.'

'How do you know, Bet? How do you know what you'd do?'

He smoothed down her plain brown hair, knowing for the thousandth time that she had none of the world's dark magic for him, and that he couldn't live without her for six consecutive hours. 'Dear Bet,' he whispered. 'Dear Bet.'

III

The Oldhornes were visiting. In the last four years, since Stuart had terminated his bondage to Gus Myers, they had become visiting people. The children visited Grandmother Van Beck during the winter and attended school in New York. Stuart and Helen visited friends in Asheville, Aiken and Palm Beach, and in the summer usually occupied a small cottage on someone's Long Island estate. 'My dear, it's just standing there empty. I wouldn't dream of accepting any rent. You'll be doing us a favour by occupying it.'

Usually, they were; they gave out a great deal of themselves in that eternal willingness and enthusiasm which makes a success-ful guest—it became their profession. Moving through a world that was growing rich with the war in Europe, Stuart had some-where lost his way. Twice playing brilliant golf in the national amateur, he accepted a job as professional at a club which his father had helped to found. He was restless and unhappy.

This weekend they were visiting a pupil of his. As a con-sequence of a mixed foursome, the Oldhornes went upstairs to dress for dinner surcharged with the unpleasant accumulation of many unsatisfactory months. In the afternoon, Stuart had played with their hostess and Helen with another man—a situation which Stuart always dreaded, because it forced him into competition with Helen. He had actually tried to miss that putt on the eighteenth—to just miss it. But the ball dropped in the cup. Helen went through the superficial motions of a good loser, but she devoted herself pointedly to her partner for the rest of the afternoon.

Their expressions still counterfeited amusement as they entered their room.

When the door closed, Helen's pleasant expression faded and she walked toward the dressing table as though her own reflection was the only decent company with which to forgather. Stuart watched her, frowning.

'I know why you're in a rotten humour,' he said; 'though I don't believe you know yourself.'

'I'm not in a rotten humour,' Helen responded in a clipped voice.

'You are; and I know the real reason—the one you don't know. It's because I holed that putt this afternoon.'

She turned slowly, incredulously, from the mirror.

'Oh, so I have a new fault! I've suddenly become, of all things, a poor sport!'

'It's not like you to be a poor sport,' he admitted, 'but other-wise why all this interest in other men, and why do you look at me as if I'm—well, slightly gamy?'

'I'm not aware of it.'

'I am.' He was aware, too, that there was always some man in their life now—some man of power and money who paid court to Helen and gave her the sense of solidity which he failed to provide. He had no cause to be jealous of any particular man, but the pressure of many was irritating. It annoyed him that on so slight a grievance, Helen should remind him by her actions that he no longer filled her entire life.

'If Anne can get any satisfaction out of winning, she's welcome to it,' said Helen suddenly.

'Isn't that rather petty? She isn't in your class; she won't qualify for the third flight in Boston.'

Feeling herself in the wrong, she changed her tone.

'Oh, that isn't it,' she broke out. 'I just keep wishing you and I could play together like we used to. And now you have to play with dubs, and get their wretched shots out of traps. Especially' —she hesitated—'especially when you're so unnecessarily gallant.'

The faint contempt in her voice, the mock jealousy that covered a growing indifference was apparent to him. There had been a time when, if he danced with another woman, Helen's stricken eyes followed him around the room.

'My gallantry is simply a matter of business,' he answered. 'Lessons have brought in three hundred a month all summer. How could I go to see you play at Boston next week, except that I'm going to coach other women?'

'And you're going to see me win,' announced Helen. 'Do you know that?'

'Naturally, I want nothing more,' Stuart said automatically. But the unnecessary defiance in her voice repelled him, and he suddenly wondered if he really cared whether she won or not.

At the same moment, Helen's mood changed and for a moment she saw the true situation—that she could play in amateur tournaments and Stuart could not, that the new cups in the rack were all hers now, that he had given up the fiercely competitive sportsmanship that had been the breath of life to him in order to provide necessary money.

'Oh, I'm so sorry for you, Stuart!' There were tears in her eyes. 'It seems such a shame that you can't do the things you love, and I can. Perhaps I oughtn't to play this summer.'

'Nonsense,' he said. 'You can't sit home and twirl your thumbs.'

She caught at this: 'You wouldn't want me to. I can't help be-

ing good at sports; you taught me nearly all I know. But I wish
I could help you.'

'Just try to remember I'm your best friend. Sometimes you act
as if we were rivals.'

She hesitated, annoyed by the truth of his words and un-
willing to concede an inch; but a wave of memories rushed over
her, and she thought how brave he was in his eked-out,
pieced-together life; she came and threw her arms around him.

'Darling, darling, things are going to be better. You'll see.'

Helen won the finals in the tournament at Boston the following week. Following around with the crowd, Stuart was very
proud of her. He hoped that instead of feeding her egotism, the
actual achievement would make things easier between them. He
hated the conflict that had grown out of their wanting the same
excellences, the same prizes from life.

Afterward he pursued her progress toward the clubhouse,
amused and a little jealous of the pack that fawned around her.
He reached the club among the last, and a steward accosted him.
'Professionals are served in the lower grill, please,' the man said.

'That's all right. My name's Oldhorne.'

He started to walk by, but the man barred his way.

'Sorry, sir. I realise that Mrs Oldhorne's playing in the match,
but my orders are to direct the professionals to the lower grill,
and I understand you are a professional.'

'Why, look here—' Stuart began, wildly angry, and stopped. A
group of people were listening. 'All right; never mind,' he said
gruffly, and turned away.

The memory of the experience rankled; it was the determining
factor that drove him, some weeks later, to a momentous decision.
For a long time he had been playing with the idea of joining the
Canadian Air Force, for service in France. He knew that his
absence would have little practical bearing on the lives of Helen
and the children; happening on some friends who were also full
of the restlessness of 1915, the matter was suddenly decided. But he
had not counted on the effect upon Helen; her reaction was not
so much one of grief or alarm, but as if she had been somehow
outwitted.

'But you might have told me!' she wailed. 'You leave me
dangling; you simply take yourself away without any warning.'

Once again Helen saw him as the bright and intolerably blinding hero, and her soul winced before him as it had when they first met. He was a warrior; for him, peace was only the interval between wars, and peace was destroying him. Here was the game of games beckoning him—Without throwing over the whole logic of their lives, there was nothing she could say.

'This is my sort of thing,' he said confidently, younger with his excitement. 'A few more years of this life and I'd go to pieces, take to drink. I've somehow lost your respect, and I've got to have that, even if I'm far away.'

She was proud of him again; she talked to everyone of his impending departure. Then, one September afternoon, she came home from the city, full of the old feeling of comradeship and bursting with news, to find him buried in an utter depression.

'Stuart,' she cried, 'I've got the—' She broke off. 'What's the matter, darling! Is something the matter?'

He looked at her dully. 'They turned me down,' he said.

'What?'

'My left eye.' He laughed bitterly. 'Where that dub cracked me with the brassie. I'm nearly blind in it.'

'Isn't there anything you can do?'

'Nothing.'

'Stuart!' She stared at him aghast. 'Stuart, and I was going to tell you! I was saving it for a surprise. Elsa Prentice has organised a Red Cross unit to serve with the French, and I joined it because I thought it would be wonderful if we both went. We've been measured for uniforms and bought our outfits, and we're sailing the end of next week.'

IV

Helen was a blurred figure among other blurred figures on a boat deck, dark against the threat of submarines. When the ship had slid out into the obscure future, Stuart walked eastward along Fifty-seventh Street. His grief at the severance of many ties was a weight he carried in his body, and he walked slowly, as if adjusting himself to it. To balance this there was a curious sensation of lightness in his mind. For the first time in twelve years he was alone, and the feeling came over him that he was alone for good; knowing Helen and knowing war, he could guess at the experiences she would go through, and he could not form any picture of a renewed life together afterward. He was discarded; she had proved the stronger at last. It seemed very strange and sad that his marriage should have such an ending.

He came to Carnegie Hall, dark after a concert, and his eye caught the name of Theodore Van Beck, large on the posted bills. As he stared at it, a green door opened in the side of the building and a group of people in evening dress came out. Stuart and Teddy were face to face before they recognised each other.

'Hello, there!' Teddy cried cordially. 'Did Helen sail?'

'Just now.'

'I met her on the street yesterday and she told me. I wanted you both to come to my concert. Well, she's quite a heroine, going off like that . . . Have you met my wife?'

Stuart and Betty smiled at each other.

'We've met.'

'And I didn't know it,' protested Teddy. 'Women need watching when they get toward their dotage . . . Look here, Stuart; we're having a few people up to the apartment. No heavy music or anything. Just supper and a few debutantes to tell me I was divine. It will do you good to come. I imagine you're missing Helen like the devil.'

'I don't think I—'

'Come along. They'll tell you you're divine too.'

Realising that the invitation was inspired by kindliness, Stuart accepted. It was the sort of gathering he had seldom attended, and he was surprised to meet so many people he knew. Teddy played the lion in a manner at once assertive and sceptical. Stuart listened as he enlarged to Mrs Cassius Ruthven on one of his favourite themes:

'People tried to make marriages co-operative and they've ended by becoming competitive. Impossible situation. Smart men will get to fight shy of ornamental women. A man ought to marry somebody who'll be grateful, like Betty here.'

'Now don't talk so much, Theodore Van Beck,' Betty interrupted. 'Since you're such a fine musician, you'd do well to express yourself with music instead of rash words.'

'I don't agree with your husband,' said Mrs Ruthven. 'English girls hunt with their men and play politics with them on absolutely equal terms, and it tends to draw them together.'

'It does not,' insisted Teddy. 'That's why English society is the most disorganised in the world. Betty and I are happy because we haven't any qualities in common at all.'

His exuberance grated on Stuart, and the success that flowed from him swung his mind back to the failure of his own life. He could not know that his life was not destined to be a failure. He could not read the fine story that three years later would be carved proud above his soldier's grave, or know that his restless body, which never spared itself in sport or danger, was destined to give him one last proud gallop at the end.

'They turned me down,' he was saying to Mrs Ruthven. 'I'll have to stick to Squadron A, unless we get drawn in.'

'So Helen's gone.' Mrs Ruthven looked at him, reminiscing. 'I'll never forget your wedding. You were both so handsome, so ideally suited to each other. Everybody spoke of it.'

Stuart remembered; for the moment it seemed that he had little else that it was fun to remember.

'Yes,' he agreed, nodding his head thoughtfully, 'I suppose we were a handsome pair.'

Suggestions for further reading

Scott Fitzgerald's stories are best read in the selections made by Malcolm Cowley for The Bodley Head *Collected Scott Fitzgerald*. They appear in volumes five and six published in 1963. They are also available in the five slim volumes which make up the Penguin edition. Among the most notable are: *The Diamond as Big as the Ritz, Bernice Bobs Her Hair, The Ice Palace* and *May-Day* from the early period; *The Rich Boy, The Last of the Belles* (Fitzgerald's farewell to the South of *The Jelly-Bean*) and the autobiographical *Basil* stories and *Babylon Revisited* (perhaps his finest story), *Family in the Wind, Crazy Sunday, Financing Finnegan, The Long Way Out* and the *Pat Hobby* stories from the last years. Arthur Mizener and Andrew Turnbull have both written biographies of the author and Mizener's *Afternoon of an Author* contains a number of interesting autobiographical pieces.

If you have enjoyed these stories, you will certainly enjoy *The Great Gatsby* (1926), Fitzgerald's masterpiece which exposes 'the greatest of all human dreams' (which has come to be known as 'the American dream'), with consummate pathos. Like much great fiction it can be appreciated on several levels, literal, dramatic, literary, moral and religious. *The Last Tycoon* (1941), even in its unfinished form, reveals the germ of a great tragic novel about a talented but sick Hollywood film director struggling with the increasing problems of his vast organisation. It also includes the most moving and tender love affair which the author ever described. *Tender is the Night* (1939) is a much revised novel about the fashionable society life enjoyed by Americans on the Riviera during the twenties. It was the least successful of the novels and Zelda's illness cannot have helped its composition. *This Side of Paradise* (1920) is now primarily of interest as a chronicle of the times.

W. Somerset Maugham (1874-1965)

In his introduction to *Creatures of Circumstance* William Somerset Maugham writes, 'I have never pretended to be anything but a story-teller. It has amused me to tell stories and I have told a great many.' This remark may seem excessively modest coming from a writer who has sold some forty million books throughout the world; who wrote twenty-seven plays between 1904 and 1933 and who once had four plays running concurrently in the West End; who has written many novels as well as travel and critical books. Nevertheless there is a deal of truth in this comment. The *Collected Stories* have been in the best-seller lists for many years and it is as a story-teller that Somerset Maugham is best loved. It is not difficult to see why.

Maugham was dedicated to the cause of fiction for enjoyment: 'The proper aim of the writer of fiction is not to instruct but to please . . . It is an abuse to use the novel as a pulpit or a platform.' Maugham rarely departed from this maxim except occasionally in *Cakes and Ale* and *The Razor's Edge,* which were curiously enough two of his most popular novels though for other reasons than their philosophical content. The short story does not permit the luxury of digression and the importance of economy in writing (which Sansom learnt as a copywriter) Maugham learnt as a dramatist. 'However brilliant a scene may be, however witty a line or profound a reflection, if it is not essential to his play the dramatist must cut it.'

One major problem for a short story-writer is the supply of source material. The novelist can expound his theme over hundreds of pages and a limited number of characters will often suffice. The storyteller needs a host of characters, themes and incidents with a wide variety of situations and backgrounds. Maugham happily never suffered from a dearth of material. 'I have sojourned in most parts of the world, and while I was writing stories I could seldom stay anywhere for any length of time without getting the material for one or two tales.' He is perhaps the most widely travelled writer in history.

He spent his childhood in Paris until his parents died, after which he lived with his uncle, the Rev Henry Macdonald Maugham, in Whitstable. After he left King's School, Canterbury, he spent a year at Heidelberg University learning languages. He spent the next five years in lodgings in London as a medical student at St Thomas's Hospital. It was here that he wrote *Liza of Lambeth,* his first novel. He then travelled in Spain before returning to Paris. During the war he served with the Ambulance Corps in France and Flanders. He transferred to the Secret Service and was sent to Switzerland and Russia. He also visited America and began his travels in the Pacific islands. After recovering from tuberculosis in a Scottish sanatorium he spent most of the next twenty years travelling to America, the Far East, the Near East, Europe, Africa, Malaya, Borneo and the Pacific Islands, returning when he wished to his home at Cap Ferrat in the South of France. When he sat down 'as a beginner of forty to write the story that is now called *Rain'*, which has incidentally been filmed several times because of its dramatic qualities, Maugham had a wealth of exotic experience to draw from. It is interesting to compare Maugham's tales of the South seas with those of Joseph Conrad. Although he travelled these islands in very different circumstances to Maugham and lacked the art of compression which gives Maugham's tales their succinctness, the world they describe is often the same.

The hallmarks of Maugham's writing are his lucid, almost matter-of-fact prose and his fluent dialogue, which largely accounted for his success as a playwright. He was almost entirely self-taught and chose Maupassant as his model. He was never entirely at ease with pure descriptive writing but had an intuitive gift for narrative. Moreover he was completely unpretentious. He knew that 'poetic flights and the great imaginative sweep were beyond his powers' and concentrated on what he could do well. Compare for instance the opening of one of Scott Fitzgerald's *Basil* stories, *Forging Ahead,* with any of the Maugham tales. 'Basil Duke Lee and Ripley Buckner Jnr sat on the Lees' front steps in the regretful gold of a late summer afternoon. Inside the house the telephone sang out with mysterious promise.' These two sentences swiftly capture the magic of the scene and create the suspense which holds the reader's attention. By comparison Maugham's prose is spare and unpoetic. The analysis of the characters is, however, shrewd and objective and the sense of irony within human behaviour omnipresent. It is the inconsistency of people's actions which provides the author with many of his telling dénouements. This 'upside-down trick' of course has its disadvantages. As Maugham explains in his essay on the short story, the pleasure of a second reading is inevitably reduced. There is a danger of the unpredictable becoming predictable.

Maugham was conscious of the fact that most people 'lead the lives that circumstances have thrust upon them' and he was fascinated by anyone who forsook the conventional paths in an attempt to mould his own destiny: eg Charles Strickland in *The Moon and Sixpence;* Larry in *The Razor's Edge;* George Bland in *The Alien Corn;* Edward Barnard in *The Fall of Edward Barnard;* Charles Battle in *The Breadwinner* and Thomas Wilson in *The Lotus Eater.* The varying degrees of success experienced by these characters makes a fascinating study. In the rather macabre tale, *The Lotus Eater,* Maugham takes the debate one stage further. What happens if you turn your back on worldly success for good and live entirely for pleasure?

Maugham's gift for compression came to the notice of the editor of the *Cosmopolitan* magazine and Maugham, by now an accomplished story-writer, agreed to write stories which were brief enough to cover two facing pages of the magazine, often leaving enough space for an illustration. Such was the profusion of material which the author had at his fingertips that in all he produced twenty-nine stories in the style of *The Escape.* Not intending to be profound, they are sometimes tragic and sometimes amusing, but always dextrous examples of the art of brevity.

Winter Cruise is one of Maugham's most charming pieces and illustrates many of the best features of his writing, notably the shrewd yet sympathetic exposure of human frailty, the characteristic underlying irony, the lively dialogue and the narrator's sense of fun. Maugham is often accused of being unemotional, which he excuses by referring to the legal background of his family, his own medical training and his natural reserve. He is also reported as having had no great regard for the fair sex, although Rosie Gann in *Cakes and Ale* and the maternal figures in certain plays would seem to contradict this. A brief acquaintance with Miss Reid makes light of both these charges.

The Lotus Eater

Most people, the vast majority in fact, lead the lives that circumstances have thrust upon them, and though some repine, looking upon themselves as round pegs in square holes, and think that if things had been different they might have made a much better showing, the greater part accept their lot, if not with serenity, at all events with resignation. They are like tram-cars travelling for ever on the selfsame rails. They go backwards and forwards, backwards and forwards, inevitably, till they can go no longer and then are sold as scrap-iron. It is not often that you find a man who has boldly taken the course of his life into his own hands. When you do, it is worth while having a good look at him.

That was why I was curious to meet Thomas Wilson. It was an interesting and a bold thing he had done. Of course the end was not yet and until the experiment was concluded it was impossible to call it successful. But from what I had heard it seemed he must be an odd sort of fellow and I thought I should like to know him. I had been told he was reserved, but I had a notion that with patience and tact I could persuade him to confide in me. I wanted to hear the facts from his own lips. People exaggerate, they love to romanticise, and I was quite prepared to discover that his story was not nearly so singular as I had been led to believe.

And this impression was confirmed when at last I made his acquaintance. It was on the Piazza in Capri, where I was spending the month of August at a friend's villa, and a little before sunset, when most of the inhabitants, native and foreign, gather together to chat with their friends in the cool of the evening. There is a terrace that overlooks the Bay of Naples, and when the sun sinks slowly into the sea the island of Ischia is silhouetted against a blaze of splendour. It is one of the most lovely sights in the world. I was standing there with my friend and host watching it, when suddenly he said:

'Look, there's Wilson.'

'Where?'

'The man sitting on the parapet, with his back to us. He's got a blue shirt on.'

I saw an undistinguished back and a small head of grey hair short and rather thin.

'I wish he'd turn round,' I said.

'He will presently.'

'Ask him to come and have a drink with us at Morgano's.'

'All right.'

The instant of overwhelming beauty had passed and the sun, like the top of an orange, was dipping into a wine-red sea. We turned round and leaning our backs against the parapet looked at the people who were sauntering to and fro. They were all talking their heads off and the cheerful noise was exhilarating. Then the church bell, rather cracked, but with a fine resonant note, began to ring. The Piazza at Capri, with its clock tower over the foot-path that leads up from the harbour, with the church up a flight of steps, is a perfect setting for an opera by Donizetti, and you felt that the voluble crowd might at any moment break out into a rattling chorus. It was charming and unreal.

I was so intent on the scene that I had not noticed Wilson get off the parapet and come towards us. As he passed us my friend stopped him.

'Hulloa, Wilson, I haven't seen you bathing the last few days.'

'I've been bathing on the other side for a change.'

My friend then introduced me. Wilson shook hands with me politely, but with indifference; a great many strangers come to Capri for a few days, or a few weeks, and I had no doubt he was constantly meeting people who came and went; and then my friend asked him to come along and have a drink with us.

'I was just going back to supper,' he said.

'Can't it wait?' I asked.

'I suppose it can,' he smiled.

Though his teeth were not very good his smile was attractive. It was gentle and kindly. He was dressed in a blue cotton shirt and a pair of grey trousers, much creased and none too clean, of a thin canvas, and on his feet he wore a pair of very old espadrilles. The get-up was picturesque, and very suitable to the place and the weather, but it did not at all go with his face. It was a lined, long face, deeply sunburned, thin-lipped, with small grey eyes rather close together and tight, neat features. The grey hair was carefully brushed. It was not a plain face, indeed in his youth Wilson might have been good-looking, but a prim one. He wore the blue shirt, open at the neck, and the grey canvas trousers, not as though they belonged to him, but as though, shipwrecked in his pyjamas, he had been fitted out with odd garments by compassionate strangers. Notwithstanding this careless attire he looked like the manager of a branch office in an insurance company, who should by rights be wearing a black coat with pepper-and-salt trousers, a white collar and an unobjectionable tie. I could very well see myself going to him to claim the insurance money when I had lost a watch, and being rather disconcerted while I answered the questions he put to me by his obvious impression, for all his politeness, that people who made such claims were either fools or knaves.

Moving off, we strolled across the Piazza and down the street till we came to Morgano's. We sat in the garden. Around us people were talking in Russian, German, Italian and English. We ordered drinks. Donna Lucia, the host's wife, waddled up and in her low, sweet voice passed the time of day with us. Though middle-aged now and portly, she had still traces of the wonderful beauty that thirty years before had driven artists to paint so many bad portraits of her. Her eyes, large and liquid, were the eyes of Hera and her smile was affectionate and gracious. We three gossiped for a while, for there is always a scandal of one sort or another in Capri to make a topic of conversation, but nothing was said of particular interest and in a little time Wilson got up and left us. Soon afterwards we strolled up to my friend's villa to dine. On the way he asked me what I had thought of Wilson.

'Nothing,' I said. 'I don't believe there's a word of truth in your story.'

'Why not?'

'He isn't the man to do that sort of thing.'

'How does anyone know what anyone is capable of?'

'I should put him down as an absolutely normal man of business who's retired on a comfortable income from gilt-edged securities. I think your story's just the ordinary Capri tittle-tattle.'

'Have it your own way,' said my friend.

We were in the habit of bathing at a beach called the Baths of Tiberius. We took a fly down the road to a certain point and then wandered through lemon groves and vineyards, noisy with cicadas and heavy with the hot smell of the sun, till we came to the top of the cliff down which a steep winding path led to the sea. A day or two later, just before we got down my friend said:

'Oh, there's Wilson back again.'

We scrunched over the beach, the only drawback to the bathing-place being that it was shingle and not sand, and as we came along Wilson saw us and waved. He was standing up, a pipe in his mouth, and he wore nothing but a pair of trunks. His body was dark brown, thin but not emaciated, and, considering his wrinkled face and grey hair, youthful. Hot from our walk, we undressed quickly and plunged at once into the water. Six feet from the shore it was thirty feet deep, but so clear that you could see the bottom. It was warm, yet invigorating.

When I got out Wilson was lying on his belly, with a towel under him reading a book. I lit a cigarette and went and sat down beside him.

'Had a nice swim?' he asked.

He put his pipe inside his book to mark the place and closing it put it down on the pebbles beside him. He was evidently willing to talk.

'Lovely,' I said. 'It's the best bathing in the world.'

'Of course people think those were the Baths of Tiberius*.' He waved his hand towards a shapeless mass of masonry that stood half in the water and half out. 'But that's all rot. It was just one of his villas, you know.'

I did. But it is just as well to let people tell you things when they want to. It disposes them kindly towards you if you suffer

---

*A Roman emperor who spent his last years, AD 27-37, on Capri.

them to impart information. Wilson gave a chuckle.

'Funny old fellow, Tiberius. Pity they're saying now there's not
a word of truth in all those stories about him.'

He began to tell me all about Tiberius. Well, I had read my
Suetonius* too and I had read histories of the Early Roman Empire, so there was nothing very new to me in what he said. But I
observed that he was not ill-read. I remarked on it.

'Oh, well, when I settled down here I was naturally interested,
and I have plenty of time for reading. When you live in a place
like this, with all its associations, it seems to make history so
actual. You might almost be living in historical times yourself.'

I should remark here that this was in 1913. The world was an
easy, comfortable place and no one could have imagined that
anything might happen seriously to disturb the serenity of
existence.

'How long have you been here?' I asked.

'Fifteen years.' He gave the blue and placid sea a glance, and a
strangely tender smile hovered on his thin lips. 'I fell in love with
the place at first sight. You've heard, I daresay, of the mythical
German who came here on the Naples boat just for lunch and a
look at the Blue Grotto and stayed forty years; well, I can't say I
exactly did that, but it's come to the same thing in the end. Only
it won't be forty years in my case. Twenty-five. Still, that's better
than a poke in the eye with a sharp stick.'

I waited for him to go on. For what he had just said looked
indeed as though there might be something after all in the singular story I had heard. But at that moment my friend came dripping
out of the water very proud of himself because he had swum a
mile, and the conversation turned to other things.

After that I met Wilson several times, either in the Piazza or
on the beach. He was amiable and polite. He was always pleased
to have a talk and I found out that he not only knew every inch
of the island but also the adjacent mainland. He had read a great
deal on all sorts of subjects, but his speciality was the history of
Rome and on this he was very well informed. He seemed to have
little imagination and to be of no more than average intelligence.
He laughed a good deal, but with restraint, and his sense of

*Suetonius describes Tiberius in *De Vita Caesarum*.

humour was tickled by simple jokes. A commonplace man. I did not forget the odd remark he had made during the first short chat we had had by ourselves, but he never so much as approached the topic again. One day on our return from the beach, dismissing the cab at the Piazza, my friend and I told the driver to be ready to take us up to Anacapri at five. We were going to climb Monte Solaro, dine at a tavern we favoured, and walk down in the moonlight. For it was full moon and the views by night were lovely. Wilson was standing by while we gave the cabman instructions, for we had given him a lift to save him the hot dusty walk, and more from politeness than for any other reason I asked him if he would care to join us.

'It's my party,' I said.

'I'll come with pleasure,' he answered.

But when the time came to set out my friend was not feeling well, he thought he had stayed too long in the water, and would not face the long and tiring walk. So I went alone with Wilson. We climbed the mountain, admired the spacious view, and got back to the inn as night was falling, hot, hungry and thirsty. We had ordered our dinner beforehand. The food was good, for Antonio was an excellent cook, and the wine came from his own vineyard. It was so light that you felt you could drink it like water and we finished the first bottle with our macaroni. By the time we had finished the second we felt that there was nothing much wrong with life. We sat in a little garden under a great vine laden with grapes. The air was exquisitely soft. The night was still and we were alone. The maid brought us *bel paese* cheese and a plate of figs. I ordered coffee and strega, which is the best liqueur they make in Italy. Wilson would not have a cigar, but lit his pipe.

'We've got plenty of time before we need start,' he said, 'the moon won't be over the hill for another hour.'

'Moon or no moon,' I said briskly, 'of course we've got plenty of time. That's one of the delights of Capri, that there's never any hurry.'

'Leisure,' he said. 'If only people knew! It's the most priceless thing a man can have and they're such fools they don't even know it's something to aim at. Work? They work for work's sake. They haven't got the brains to realise that the only object of work is to obtain leisure.'

Wine has the effect on some people of making them indulge in general reflections. These remarks were true, but no one could have claimed that they were original. I did not say anything, but struck a match to light my cigar.

'It was full moon the first time I came to Capri,' he went on reflectively. 'It might be the same moon as to-night.'

'It was, you know,' I smiled.

He grinned. The only light in the garden was what came from an oil lamp that hung over our heads. It had been scanty to eat by, but it was good now for confidences.

'I didn't mean that. I mean, it might be yesterday. Fifteen years it is, and when I look back it seems like a month. I'd never been to Italy before. I came for my summer holiday. I went to Naples by boat from Marseilles and I had a look round, Pompeii, you know, and Paestum and one or two places like that; then I came here for a week. I liked the look of the place right away, from the sea, I mean, as I watched it come closer and closer; and then when we got into the little boats from the steamer and landed at the quay, with all that crowd of jabbering people who wanted to take your luggage, and the hotel touts, and the tumbledown houses on the Marina and the walk up to the hotel, and dining on the terrace—well, it just got me. That's the truth. I didn't know if I was standing on my head or my heels. I'd never drunk Capri wine before, but I'd heard of it; I think I must have got a bit tight. I sat on that terrace after they'd all gone to bed and watched the moon over the sea, and there was Vesuvius with a great red plume of smoke rising up from it. Of course I know now that wine I drank was ink, Capri wine my eye, but I thought it all right then. But it wasn't the wine that made me drunk, it was the shape of the island and those jabbering people, the moon and the sea and the oleander in the hotel garden. I'd never seen an oleander before.'

It was a long speech and it had made him thirsty. He took up his glass, but it was empty. I asked him if he would have another strega.

'It's sickly stuff. Let's have a bottle of wine. That's sound, that is, pure juice of the grape and can't hurt anyone.'

I ordered more wine, and when it came filled the glasses. He took a long drink and after a sigh of pleasure went on.

'Next day I found my way to the bathing-place we go to. Not bad bathing, I thought. Then I wandered about the island. As luck would have it, there was a *festa* up at the Punta di Timberio and I ran straight into the middle of it. An image of the Virgin and priests, acolytes swinging censers, and a whole crowd of jolly, laughing, excited people, a lot of them all dressed up. I ran across an Englishman there and asked him what it was all about. "Oh, it's the feast of the Assumption," he said, "at least that's what the Catholic Church says it is, but that's just their hanky-panky. It's the festival of Venus. Pagan, you know. Aphrodite rising from the sea and all that." It gave me quite a funny feeling to hear him. It seemed to take one a long way back, if you know what I mean. After that I went down one night to have a look at the Faraglioni by moonlight. If the fates had wanted me to go on being a bank manager they oughtn't to have let me take that walk.'

'You were a bank manager, were you?' I asked.

I had been wrong about him, but not far wrong.

'Yes. I was manager of the Crawford Street branch of the York and City. It was convenient for me because I lived up Hendon way. I could get from door to door in thirty-seven minutes.'

He puffed at his pipe and relit it.

'That was my last night, that was. I'd got to be back at the bank on Monday morning. When I looked at those two great rocks sticking out of the water, with the moon above them, and all the little lights of the fishermen in their boats catching cuttle-fish, all so peaceful and beautiful, I said to myself, well, after all, why should I go back? It wasn't as if I had anyone dependent on me. My wife had died of bronchial pneumonia four years before and the kid went to live with her grandmother, my wife's mother. She was an old fool, she didn't look after the kid properly and she got blood-poisoning, they amputated her leg, but they couldn't save her and she died, poor little thing.'

'How terrible,' I said.

'Yes, I was cut up at the time, though of course not so much as if the kid had been living with me, but I dare say it was a mercy. Not much chance for a girl with only one leg. I was sorry about my wife too. We got on very well together. Though I don't know if it would have continued. She was the sort of woman who was always bothering about what other people'd think. She didn't like travelling. Eastbourne was her idea of a holiday. D'you know, I'd never crossed the Channel till after her death.'

'But I suppose you've got other relations, haven't you?'

'None. I was an only child. My father had a brother, but he went to Australia before I was born. I don't think anyone could easily be more alone in the world than I am. There wasn't any reason I could see why I shouldn't do exactly what I wanted. I was thirty-four at that time.'

He had told me he had been on the island for fifteen years. That would make him forty-nine. Just about the age I should have given him.

'I'd been working since I was seventeen. All I had to look forward to was doing the same old thing day after day till I retired on my pension. I said to myself, is it worth it? What's wrong with chucking it all up and spending the rest of my life down here? It was the most beautiful place I'd ever seen. But I'd had a business training, I was cautious by nature. "No," I said, "I won't be carried away like this, I'll go tomorrow like I said I would and think it over. Perhaps when I get back to London I'll think differently." Damned fool, wasn't I? I lost a whole year that way.'

'You didn't change your mind, then?'

'You bet I didn't. All the time I was working I kept thinking of the bathing here and the vineyards and the walks over the hills and the moon and the sea, and the Piazza in the evening when everyone walks about for a bit of a chat after the day's work is over. There was only one thing that bothered me: I wasn't sure if I was justified in not working like everybody else did. Then I read a sort of history book, by a man called Marion Crawford* it was, and there was a story about Sybaris and Crotona. There were two cities; and in Sybaris they just enjoyed life and had a good time, and in Crotona they were hardy and industrious and all that. And one day the men of Crotona came over and wiped Sybaris out, and then after a while a lot of other fellows came over from somewhere else and wiped Crotona out. Nothing remains of Sybaris, not a stone, and all that's left of Crotona is just one column.

*American author (1854-1909) who settled in Sorrento.

That settled the matter for me.'

'Oh?'

'It came to the same in the end, didn't it? And when you look back now, who were the mugs?'

I did not reply and he went on.

'The money was rather a bother. The bank didn't pension one off till after thirty years' service, but if you retired before that they gave you a gratuity. With that and what I'd got for the sale of my house and the little I'd managed to save, I just hadn't enough to buy an annuity to last the rest of my life. It would have been silly to sacrifice everything so as to lead a pleasant life and not have a sufficient income to make it pleasant. I wanted to have a little place of my own, a servant to look after me, enough to buy tobacco, decent food, books now and then, and something over for emergencies. I knew pretty well how much I needed. I found I had just enough to buy an annuity for twenty-five years.'

'You were thirty-five at the time?'

'Yes. It would carry me on till I was sixty. After all, no one can be certain of living longer than that, a lot of men die in their fifties, and by the time a man's sixty he's had the best of life.'

'On the other hand no one can be sure of dying at sixty,' I said.

'Well, I don't know. It depends on himself, doesn't it?'

'In your place I should have stayed on at the bank till I was entitled to my pension.'

'I should have been forty-seven then. I shouldn't have been too old to enjoy my life here, I'm older than that now and I enjoy it as much as I ever did, but I should have been too old to experience the particular pleasure of a young man. You know, you can have just as good a time at fifty as you can at thirty, but it's not the same sort of good time. I wanted to live the perfect life while I still had the energy and the spirit to make the most of it. Twenty-five years seemed a long time to me, and twenty-five years of happiness seemed worth paying something pretty substantial for. I'd made up my mind to wait a year and I waited a year. Then I sent in my resignation and as soon as they paid me my gratuity I bought the annuity and came on here.'

'An annuity for twenty-five years?'

'That's right.'

'Have you never regretted?'

'Never. I've had my money's worth already. And I've got ten years more. Don't you think after twenty-five years of perfect happiness one ought to be satisfied to call it a day?'

'Perhaps.'.

He did not say in so many words what he would do then, but his intention was clear. It was pretty much the story my friend had told me, but it sounded different when I heard it from his own lips. I stole a glance at him. There was nothing about him that was not ordinary. No one, looking at that neat, prim face, could have thought him capable of an unconventional action. I did not blame him. It was his own life that he had arranged in this strange manner, and I did not see why he should not do what he liked with it. Still, I could not prevent the little shiver that ran down my spine.

'Getting chilly?' he smiled. 'We might as well start walking down. The moon'll be up by now.'

Before we parted Wilson asked me if I would like to go and see his house one day; and two or three days later, finding out where he lived, I strolled up to see him. It was a peasant's cottage, well away from the town, in a vineyard, with a view of the sea. By the side of the door grew a great oleander in full flower. There were only two small rooms, a tiny kitchen and a lean-to in which firewood could be kept. The bedroom was furnished like a monk's cell, but the sitting-room, smelling agreeably of tobacco, was comfortable enough, with two large arm-chairs that he had brought from England, a large roll-top desk, a cottage piano and crowded bookshelves. On the walls were framed engravings of pictures by G.F. Watts and Lord Leighton. Wilson told me that the house belonged to the owner of the vineyard who lived in another cottage higher up the hill, and his wife came in every day to do the rooms and the cooking. He had found the place on his first visit to Capri, and taking it on his return for good had been there ever since. Seeing the piano and music open on it, I asked him if he would play.

'I'm no good, you know, but I've always been fond of music and I get a lot of fun out of strumming.'

He sat down at the piano and played one of the movements from a Beethoven sonata. He did not play very well. I looked at his music, Schumann and Schubert, Beethoven, Bach and Chopin. On the table on which he had his meals was a greasy pack of cards. I asked him if he played patience.

'A lot.'

From what I saw of him then and from what I heard from other people I made for myself what I think must have been a fairly accurate picture of the life he had led for the last fifteen years. It was certainly a very harmless one. He bathed; he walked a great deal, and he seemed never to lose his sense of the beauty of the island which he knew so intimately; he played the piano and he played patience; he read. When he was asked to a party he went and, though a trifle dull, was agreeable. He was not affronted if he was neglected. He liked people, but with an aloofness that prevented intimacy. He lived thriftily, but with sufficient comfort. He never owed a penny. I imagine he had never been a man whom sex had greatly troubled, and if in his younger days he had had now and then a passing affair with a visitor to the island whose head was turned by the atmosphere, his emotion, while it lasted, remained, I am pretty sure, well under his control. I think he was determined that nothing should interfere with his independence of spirit. His only passion was for the beauty of nature, and he sought felicity in the simple and natural things that life offers to everyone. You may say that it was a grossly selfish existence. It was. He was of no use to anybody, but on the other hand he did nobody any harm. His only object was his own happiness, and it looked as though he had attained it. Very few people know where to look for happiness; fewer still find it. I don't know whether he was a fool or a wise man. He was certainly a man who knew his own mind. The odd thing about him to me was that he was so immensely commonplace. I should never have given him a second thought but for what I knew, that on a certain day, ten years from then, unless a chance illness cut the thread before, he must deliberately take leave of the world he loved so well. I wondered whether it was the thought of this, never quite absent from his mind, that gave him the peculiar zest with which he enjoyed every moment of the day.

I should do him an injustice if I omitted to state that he was not at all in the habit of talking about himself. I think the friend I was staying with was the only person in whom he had confided.

I believe he only told me the story because he suspected I already knew it, and on the evening on which he told it to me he had drunk a good deal of wine.

My visit drew to a close and I left the island. The year after, war broke out. A number of things happened to me, so that the course of my life was greatly altered, and it was thirteen years before I went to Capri again. My friend had been back some time, but he was no longer so well off, and had moved into a house that had no room for me; so I was putting up at the hotel. He came to meet me at the boat and we dined together. During dinner I asked him where exactly his house was.

'You know it,' he answered. 'It's the little place Wilson had. I've built on a room and made it quite nice.'

With so many other things to occupy my mind I had not given Wilson a thought for years; but now, with a little shock, I remembered. The ten years he had before him when I made his acquaintance must have elapsed long ago.

'Did he commit suicide as he said he would?'

'It's rather a grim story.'

Wilson's plan was all right. There was only one flaw in it and this, I suppose, he could not have foreseen. It had never occurred to him that after twenty-five years of complete happiness, in this quiet backwater, with nothing in the world to disturb his serenity, his character would gradually lose its strength. The will needs obstacles in order to exercise its power; when it is never thwarted, when no effort is needed to achieve one's desires, because one has placed one's desires only in the things that can be obtained by stretching out one's hand, the will grows impotent. If you walk on a level all the time the muscles you need to climb a mountain will atrophy. These observations are trite, but there they are. When Wilson's annuity expired he had no longer the resolution to make the end which was the price he had agreed to pay for that long period of happy tranquillity. I do not think, as far as I could gather, both from what my friend told me and afterwards from others, that he wanted courage. It was just that he couldn't make up his mind. He put it off from day to day.

He had lived on the island for so long and had always settled his accounts so punctually that it was easy for him to get credit; never having borrowed money before, he found a number of people who were willing to lend him small sums when now he asked for them. He had paid his rent regularly for so many years that his landlord, whose wife Assunta still acted as his servant, was content to let things slide for several months. Everyone believed him when he said that a relative had died and that he was temporarily embarrassed because owing to legal formalities he could not for some time get the money that was due to him. He managed to hang on after this fashion for something over a year. Then he could get no more credit from the local tradesmen, and there was no one to lend him any more money. His landlord gave him notice to leave the house unless he paid up the arrears of rent before a certain date.

The day before this he went into his tiny bedroom, closed the door and the window, drew the curtain and lit a brazier of charcoal. Next morning when Assunta came to make his breakfast she found him insensible but still alive. The room was draughty, and though he had done this and that to keep out the fresh air he had not done it very thoroughly. It almost looked as though at the last moment, and desperate though his situation was, he had suffered from a certain infirmity of purpose. Wilson was taken to the hospital, and though very ill for some time he at last recovered. But as a result either of the charcoal poisoning or of the shock he was no longer in complete possession of his faculties. He was not insane, at all events not insane enough to be put in an asylum, but he was quite obviously no longer in his right mind.

'I went to see him,' said my friend. 'I tried to get him to talk, but he kept looking at me in a funny sort of way, as though he couldn't quite make out where he'd seen me before. He looked rather awful lying there in bed, with a week's growth of grey beard on his chin; but except for that funny look in his eyes he seemed quite normal.'

'What funny look in his eyes?'

'I don't know exactly how to describe it. Puzzled. It's an absurd comparison, but suppose you threw a stone up into the air and it didn't come down but just stayed there . . .'

'It would be rather bewildering,' I smiled.

'Well, that's the sort of look he had.'

It was difficult to know what to do with him. He had no money and no means of getting any. His effects were sold, but for too little to pay what he owed. He was English, and the Italian authorities did not wish to make themselves responsible for him. The British Consul in Naples had no funds to deal with the case. He could of course be sent back to England, but no one seemed to know what could be done with him when he got there. Then Assunta, the servant, said that he had been a good master and a good tenant, and as long as he had the money had paid his way; he could sleep in the woodshed in the cottage in which she and her husband lived, and he could share their meals. This was suggested to him. It was difficult to know whether he understood or not. When Assunta came to take him from the hospital he went with her without remark. He seemed to have no longer a will of his own. She had been keeping him now for two years.

'It's not very comfortable, you know,' said my friend. 'They've rigged him up a ramshackle bed and given him a couple of blankets, but there's no window, and it's icy cold in winter and like an oven in summer. And the food's pretty rough. You know how these peasants eat: macaroni on Sundays and meat once in a blue moon.'

'What does he do with himself all the time?'

'He wanders about the hills. I've tried to see him two or three times, but it's no good; when he sees you coming he runs like a hare. Assunta comes down to have a chat with me now and then and I give her a bit of money so that she can buy him tobacco, but God knows if he ever gets it.'

'Do they treat him all right?' I asked.

'I'm sure Assunta's kind enough. She treats him like a child. I'm afraid her husband's not very nice to him. He grudges the cost of his keep. I don't believe he's cruel or anything like that, but I think he's a bit sharp with him. He makes him fetch water and clean the cow-shed and that sort of thing.'

'It sounds pretty rotten,' I said.

'He brought it on himself. After all, he's only got what he deserved.'

'I think on the whole we all get what we deserve,' I said. 'But that doesn't prevent its being rather horrible.'

Two or three days later my friend and I were taking a walk. We were strolling along a narrow path through an olive grove.

'There's Wilson,' said my friend suddenly. 'Don't look, you'll only frighten him. Go straight on.'

I walked with my eyes on the path, but out of the corners of them I saw a man hiding behind an olive tree. He did not move as we approached, but I felt that he was watching us. As soon as we had passed I heard a scamper. Wilson, like a hunted animal, had made for safety. That was the last I ever saw of him.

He died last year. He had endured that life for six years. He was found one morning on the mountainside lying quite peacefully as though he had died in his sleep. From where he lay he had been able to see those two great rocks called the Faraglioni which stand out of the sea. It was full moon and he must have gone to see them by moonlight. Perhaps he died of the beauty of that sight.

The Escape

I have always been convinced that if a woman once made up her mind to marry a man nothing but instant flight could save him. Not always that; for once a friend of mine, seeing the inevitable loom menacingly before him, took ship from a certain port (with a tooth-brush for all his luggage, so conscious was he of his danger and the necessity for immediate action) and spent a year travelling round the world; but when, thinking himself safe (women are fickle, he said, and in twelve months she will have forgotten all about me), he landed at the selfsame port the first person he saw gaily waving to him from the quay was the little lady from whom he had fled. I have only once known a man who in such circumstances managed to extricate himself. His name was Roger Charing. He was no longer young when he fell in love with Ruth Barlow and he had had sufficient experience to make him careful; but Ruth Barlow had a gift (or should I call it a quality?) that renders most men defenceless, and it was this that dispossessed Roger of his commonsense, his prudence and his worldly wisdom. He went down like a row of ninepins. This was the gift of pathos. Mrs Barlow, for she was twice a widow, had splendid dark eyes and they were the most moving I ever saw; they seemed to be ever on the point of filling with tears; they suggested that the world was too much for her, and you felt that, poor dear, her sufferings had been more than anyone should be asked to bear. If, like Roger Charing, you were a strong, hefty fellow with plenty of money, it was almost inevitable that you should say to yourself: I must stand between the hazards of life and this helpless little thing, oh, how wonderful it would be to take the sadness out of those big and lovely eyes! I gathered from Roger that everyone had treated Mrs Barlow very badly. She was apparently one of those unfortunate persons with whom nothing by any chance goes right. If she married a husband he beat her; if she employed a broker he cheated her; if she engaged a cook she drank. She never had a little lamb but it was sure to die.

When Roger told me that he had at last persuaded her to marry him, I wished him joy.

'I hope you'll be good friends,' he said. 'She's a little afraid of you, you know; she thinks you're callous.'

'Upon my word I don't know why she should think that.'

'You do like her, don't you?'

'Very much.'

'She's had a rotten time, poor dear. I feel so dreadfully sorry for her.'

'Yes,' I said.

I couldn't say less. I knew she was stupid and I thought she was scheming. My own belief was that she was as hard as nails.

The first time I met her we had played bridge together and when she was my partner she twice trumped my best card. I behaved like an angel, but I confess that I thought if the tears were going to well up into anybody's eyes they should have been mine rather than hers. And when, having by the end of the evening lost a good deal of money to me, she said she would send me a cheque and never did, I could not but think that I and not she should have worn a pathetic expression when next we met.

Roger introduced her to his friends. He gave her lovely jewels. He took her here, there and everywhere. Their marriage was announced for the immediate future. Roger was very happy. He was committing a good action and at the same time doing something he had very much a mind to do. It is an uncommon situation and it is not surprising if he was a trifle more pleased with himself than was altogether becoming.

Then, on a sudden, he fell out of love. I do not know why. It could hardly have been that he grew tired of her conversation, for she had never had any conversation. Perhaps it was merely that this pathetic look of hers ceased to wring his heart-strings. His eyes were opened and he was once more the shrewd man of the world he had been. He became acutely conscious that Ruth Barlow had made up her mind to marry him and he swore a solemn oath that nothing would induce him to marry Ruth Barlow. But he was in a quandary. Now that he was in possession of his senses he saw with clearness the sort of woman he had to deal with and he was aware that, if he asked her to release him, she would (in her appealing way) assess her wounded feelings at an immoderately high figure. Besides, it is always awkward for a man to jilt a woman. People are apt to think he has behaved badly.

Roger kept his own counsel. He gave neither by word nor gesture an indication that his feelings towards Ruth Barlow had changed. He remained attentive to all her wishes; he took her to dine at restaurants, they went to the play together, he sent her flowers; he was sympathetic and charming. They had made up their minds that they would be married as soon as they found a house that suited them, for he lived in chambers and she in furnished rooms; and they set about looking at desirable residences. The agents sent Roger orders to view and he took Ruth to see a number of houses. It was very hard to find anything that was quite satisfactory. Roger applied to more agents. They visited house after house. They went over them thoroughly, examining them from the cellars in the basement to the attics under the roof. Sometimes they were too large and sometimes they were too small; sometimes they were too far from the centre of things and sometimes they were too close; sometimes they were too expensive and sometimes they wanted too many repairs; sometimes they were too stuffy and sometimes they were too airy; sometimes they were too dark and sometimes they were too bleak. Roger always found a fault that made the house unsuitable. Of course he was hard to please; he could not bear to ask his dear Ruth to live in any but the perfect house, and the perfect house wanted finding. House-hunting is a tiring and a tiresome business and presently Ruth began to grow peevish. Roger begged her to have patience;

somewhere, surely, existed the very house they were looking for and it only needed a little perseverance and they would find it. They looked at hundreds of houses; they climbed thousands of stairs; they inspected innumerable kitchens. Ruth was exhausted and more than once lost her temper.

'If you don't find a house soon,' she said, 'I shall have to reconsider my position. Why, if you go on like this we shan't be married for years.'

'Don't say that,' he answered, 'I beseech you to have patience. I've just received some entirely new lists from agents I've only just heard of. There must be at least sixty houses on them.'

They set out on the chase again. They looked at more houses and more houses. For two years they looked at houses. Ruth grew silent and scornful: her pathetic, beautiful eyes acquired an expression that was almost sullen. There are limits to human endurance. Mrs Barlow had the patience of an angel, but at last she revolted.

'Do you want to marry me or do you not?' she asked him.

There was an unaccustomed hardness in her voice, but it did not affect the gentleness of his reply.

'Of course I do. We'll be married the very moment we find a house. By the way, I've just heard of something that might suit us.'

'I don't feel well enough to look at any more houses just yet.'

'Poor dear, I was afraid you were looking rather tired.'

Ruth Barlow took to her bed. She would not see Roger and he had to content himself with calling at her lodgings to enquire and sending her flowers. He was as ever assiduous and gallant. Every day he wrote and told her that he had heard of another house for them to look at. A week passed and then he received the following letter:

Roger,

I do not think you really love me. I have found someone who is anxious to take care of me and I am going to be married to him to-day.

Ruth.

He sent back his reply by special messenger:

Ruth,

Your news shatters me. I shall never get over the blow, but of course your happiness must be my first consideration. I send you herewith seven orders to view; they arrived by this morning's post and I am quite sure you will find among them a house that will exactly suit you.

Roger.

Winter Cruise

Captain Erdmann knew Miss Reid very little till the *Friedrich Weber* reached Haiti. She came on board at Plymouth, but by then he had taken on a number of passengers, French, Belgian and Haitian, many of whom had travelled with him before, and she was placed at the chief engineer's table. The *Friedrich Weber* was a freighter sailing regularly from Hamburg to Cartagena on the Columbian coast and on the way touching at a number of islands in the West Indies. She carried phosphates and cement from Germany and took back coffee and timber; but her owners, the Brothers Weber, were always willing to send her out of her route if a cargo of any sort made it worth their while. The *Friedrich Weber* was prepared to take cattle, mules, potatoes or anything else that offered the chance of earning an honest penny. She carried passengers. There were six cabins on the upper deck and six below. The accommodation was not luxurious, but the food was good, plain and abundant, and the fares were cheap. The round trip took nine weeks and was not costing Miss Reid more than forty-five pounds. She looked forward not only to seeing many interesting places, with historical associations, but also to acquiring a great deal of information that would enrich her mind.

The agent had warned her that till the ship reached Port au Prince in Haiti she would have to share her cabin with another woman. Miss Reid did not mind that, she liked company, and when the steward told her that her companion was Madame Bollin she thought at once that it would be a very good opportunity to rub up her French. She was only very slightly disconcerted when she found that Madame Bollin was coal-black. She told herself that one had to accept the rough with the smooth and that it takes all sorts to make a world. Miss Reid was a good sailor, as indeed was only to be expected since her grandfather had been a naval officer, but after a couple of roughish days the weather was fine and in a very short while she knew all her fellow-passengers. She was a good mixer. That was one of the reasons why she had made a success of her business; she owned a tea-room at a celebrated beauty spot in the west of England and she always had a smile and a pleasant word for every customer who came in; she closed down in the winter and for the last four years had taken a cruise. You met such interesting people, she said, and you always learnt something. It was true that the passengers on the *Friedrich Weber* weren't of quite so good a class as those she had met the year before on her Mediterranean cruise, but Miss Reid was not a snob, and though the table manners of some of them shocked her somewhat, determined to look upon the bright side of things she decided to make the best of them. She was a great reader and she was glad, on looking at the ship's library, to find that there were a lot of books by Phillips Oppenheim, Edgar Wallace and Agatha Christie; but with so many people to talk to she had no time for reading and she made up her mind to leave them till the ship emptied herself at Haiti.

'After all,' she said, 'human nature is more important than literature.'

Miss Reid had always had the reputation of being a good talker and she flattered herself that not once during the many days they were at sea had she allowed the conversation at table to languish. She knew how to draw people out, and whenever a topic seemed to be exhausted she had a remark ready to revive it or another topic waiting on the tip of her tongue to set the conversation off again. Her friend Miss Prince, daughter of the late Vicar of Campden, who had come to see her off at Plymouth, for she lived there, had often said to her:

'You know, Venetia, you have a mind like a man. You're never at a loss for something to say.'

'Well, I think if you're interested in everyone, everyone will be interested in you,' Miss Reid answered modestly. 'Practice makes perfect, and I have the infinite capacity for taking pains which

Dickens said was genius.'

Miss Reid was not really called Venetia, her name was Alice, but disliking it she had, when still a girl, adopted the poetic name which she felt so much better suited to her personality.

Miss Reid had a great many interesting talks with her fellow-passengers and she was really sorry when the ship at length reached Port au Prince and the last of them disembarked. The *Friedrich Weber* stopped two days there, during which she visited the town and the neighbourhood. When they sailed she was the only passenger. The ship was skirting the coast of the island stopping off at a variety of ports to discharge or to take on cargo.

'I hope you will not feel embarrassed alone with so many men, Miss Reid,' said the captain heartily as they sat down to midday dinner.

She was placed on his right hand and at table besides sat the first mate, the chief engineer and the doctor.

'I'm a woman of the world, Captain. I always think if a lady is a lady gentlemen will be gentlemen.'

'We're only rough sailor men, madam, you mustn't expect too much.'

'Kind hearts are more than coronets and simple faith than Norman blood, Captain,' answered Miss Reid.

He was a short, thick-set man, with a clean-shaven head and a red, clean-shaven face. He wore a white stingah-shifter, but except at meal-times unbuttoned at the neck and showing his hairy chest. He was a jovial fellow. He could not speak without bellowing. Miss Reid thought him quite an eccentric, but she had a keen sense of humour and was prepared to make allowances for that. She took the conversation in hand. She had learnt a great deal about Haiti on the voyage out and more during the two days she had spent there, but she knew that men liked to talk rather than to listen, so she put them a number of questions to which she already knew the answers; oddly enough they didn't. In the end she found herself obliged to give quite a little lecture, and before dinner was over, *Mittag Essen* they called it in their funny way, she had imparted to them a great deal of interesting information about the history and economic situation of the Republic, the problems that confronted it and its prospects for the future. She talked rather slowly, in a refined voice, and her vocabulary was extensive.

At nightfall they put in at a small port where they were to load three hundred bags of coffee, and the agent came on board. The captain asked him to stay to supper and ordered cocktails. As the steward brought them Miss Reid swam into the saloon. Her movements were deliberate, elegant and self-assured. She always said that you could tell at once by the way she walked if a woman was a lady. The captain introduced the agent to her and she sat down.

'What is that you men are drinking?' she asked.

'A cocktail. Will you have one, Miss Reid?'

'I don't mind if I do.'

She drank it and the captain somewhat doubtfully asked her if she would have another.

'Another? Well, just to be matey.'

The agent, much whiter than some, but a good deal darker than many, was the son of a former minister of Haiti to the German court, and having lived for many years in Berlin spoke good German. It was indeed on this account that he had got a job with a German shipping firm. On the strength of this Miss Reid, during supper, told them all about a trip down the Rhine that she had once taken. Afterwards she and the agent, the skipper, the doctor and the mate, sat round a table and drank beer. Miss Reid made it her business to draw the agent out. The fact that they were loading coffee suggested to her that he would be interested in learning how they grew tea in Ceylon, yes, she had been to Ceylon on a cruise, and the fact that his father was a diplomat made it certain that he would be interested in the royal family of England. She had a very pleasant evening. When she at last retired to rest, for she would never have thought of saying she was going to bed, she said to herself:

'There's no doubt that travel is a great education.'

It was really an experience to find herself alone with all those men. How they would laugh when she told them all about it when she got home! They would say that things like that only happened to Venetia. She smiled when she heard the captain on deck singing with that great booming voice of his. Germans were so musical. He had a funny way of strutting up and down on his short legs singing Wagner tunes to words of his own invention. It was *Tannhaüser* he was singing now (that lovely thing about the evening star*) but knowing no German Miss Reid could only wonder what absurd words he was putting to it. It was as well.

'Oh, what a bore that woman is, I shall certainly kill her if she goes on much longer.' Then he broke into Siegfried's martial strain. 'She's a bore, she's a bore, she's a bore. I shall throw her into the sea.'

And that of course is what Miss Reid was. She was a crashing, she was a stupendous, she was an excruciating bore. She talked in a steady monotone and it was no use to interrupt her because then she started again from the beginning. She had an insatiable thirst for information and no casual remark could be thrown across the table without her asking innumerable questions about it. She was a great dreamer and she narrated her dreams at intolerable length. There was no subject upon which she had not something prosy to say. She had a truism for every occasion. She hit on the commonplace like a hammer driving a nail into the wall. She plunged into the obvious like a clown in a circus jumping through a hoop. Silence did not abash her. Those poor men far away from their homes and the patter of little feet, and with Christmas coming on, no wonder they felt low; she redoubled her efforts to interest and amuse them. She was determined to bring a little gaiety into their dull lives. For that was the awful part of it: Miss Reid meant well. She was not only having a good time herself, but she was trying to give all of them a good time. She was convinced that they liked her as much as she liked them. She felt that she was doing her bit to make the party a success and she was naïvely happy to think that she was succeeding. She told them all about her friend Miss Price and how often she had said to her: Venetia, no one ever has a dull moment in your company. It was the captain's duty to be polite to a passenger, and however much he would have liked to tell her to hold her silly tongue he could not, but even if he had been free to say what he liked, he knew that he could not have brought himself to hurt her feelings. Nothing stemmed the torrent of her loquacity. It was as irresistible as a force of nature. Once in desperation they

*'O du mein holder Abendstern,' Walfrum's tender and beautiful prayer to the evening star to protect Elizabeth. (Ironically enough this aria is also a confession of love for her.)

began talking German, but Miss Reid stopped this at once.

'Now I won't have you saying things I don't understand. You ought all to make the most of your good luck in having me all to yourselves and practise your English.'

'We were talking of technical matters that would only bore you, Miss Reid,' said the captain.

'I'm never bored. That's why, if you won't think me a wee bit conceited to say so, I'm never boring. You see, I like to know things. Everything interests me and you never know when a bit of information won't come in useful.'

The doctor smiled drily.

'The captain was only saying that because he was embarrassed. In point of fact he was telling a story that was not fit for the ears of a maiden lady.'

'I may be a maiden lady but I'm also a woman of the world, I don't expect sailors to be saints. You need never be afraid of what you say before me, Captain, I shan't be shocked. I should love to hear your story.'

The doctor was a man of sixty with thin grey hair, a grey moustache and small bright blue eyes. He was a silent, bitter man, and however hard Miss Reid tried to bring him into the conversation it was almost impossible to get a word out of him. But she wasn't a woman who would give in without a struggle, and one morning when they were at sea and she saw him sitting on deck with a book, she brought her chair next to his and sat down beside him.

'Are you fond of reading, Doctor?' she said brightly.

'Yes.'

'So am I. And I suppose like all Germans you're musical.'

'I'm fond of music.'

So am I. The moment I saw you I thought you looked clever.'

He gave her a brief look and pursing his lips went on reading. Miss Reid was not disconcerted.

'But of course one can always read. I always prefer a good talk to a good book. Don't you?'

'No.'

'How interesting. Now do tell me why?'

'I can't give you a reason.'

'That's very strange, isn't it? But then I always think human nature is strange. I'm terribly interested in people, you know. I always like doctors, they know so much about human nature, but I could tell you some things that would surprise even you. You learn a great deal about people if you run a tea-shop like I do, that's to say if you keep your eyes open.'

The doctor got up.

'I must ask you to excuse me, Miss Reid. I have to go and see a patient.'

'Anyhow I've broken the ice now,' she thought, as he walked away. 'I think he was only shy.'

But a day or two later the doctor was not feeling at all well. He had an internal malady that troubled him now and then, but he was used to it and disinclined to talk about it. When he had one of his attacks he only wanted to be left alone. His cabin was small and stuffy, so he settled himself on a long chair on deck and lay with his eyes closed. Miss Reid was walking up and down to get the half-hour's exercise she took morning and evening. He thought that if he pretended to be asleep she would not disturb him. But when she had passed him half a dozen times she stopped in front of him and stood quite still. Though he kept his eyes closed he knew that she was looking at him.

'Is there anything I can do, Doctor?' she said.

He started.

'Why, what should there be?'

He gave her a glance and saw that her eyes were deeply troubled.

'You look dreadfully ill,' she said.

'I'm in great pain.'

'I know. I can see that. Can't something be done?'

'No, it'll pass off presently.'

She hesitated for a moment then went away. Presently she returned.

'You look so uncomfortable with no cushions or anything. I've brought you my own pillow that I always travel with. Do let me put it behind your head.'

He felt at that moment too ill to remonstrate. She lifted his head gently and put the soft pillow behind it. It really did make him feel more comfortable. She passed her hand across his forehead and it was cool and soft.

'Poor dear,' she said. 'I know what doctors are. They haven't the first idea how to take care of themselves.'

She left him, but in a minute or two returned with a chair and a bag. The doctor when he saw her gave a twitch of anguish.

'Now I'm not going to let you talk, I'm just going to sit beside you and knit. I always think it's a comfort when one isn't feeling very well to have someone near.'

She sat down and taking an unfinished muffler out of her bag began busily to ply her needles. She never said a word. And strangely enough the doctor found her company a solace. No one else on board had even noticed that he was ill, he had felt lonely, and the sympathy of that crashing bore was grateful to him. It soothed him to see her silently working and presently he fell asleep. When he awoke she was still working. She gave him a little smile, but did not speak. His pain had left him and he felt much better.

He did not go into the saloon till late in the afternoon. He found the captain and Hans Krause, the mate, having a glass of beer together.

'Sit down, Doctor,' said the captain. 'We're holding a council of war. You know that the day after tomorrow is Sylvester Abend.'

'Of course.'

'Sylvester Abend, New Year's Eve, is an occasion that means a great deal to a German and they had all been looking forward to it. They had brought a Christmas tree all the way from Germany with them.

'At dinner today Miss Reid was more talkative than ever. Hans and I have decided that something must be done about it.'

'She sat with me for two hours this morning in silence. I suppose she was making up for lost time.'

'It's bad enough to be away from one's home and family just now anyway and all we can do is to make the best of a bad job. We want to enjoy our Sylvester Abend, and unless something is done about Miss Reid we haven't a chance.'

'We can't have a good time if she's with us,' said the mate. 'She'll spoil it as sure as eggs is eggs.'

'How do you propose to get rid of her, short of throwing her overboard?' smiled the doctor. 'She's not a bad old soul; all she wants is a lover.'

'At her age?' cried Hans Krause.

'Especially at her age. That inordinate loquacity, that passion for information, the innumerable questions she asks, her prosiness, the way she goes on and on—it is all a sign of her clamouring virginity. A lover would bring her peace. Those jangled nerves of hers would relax. At least for an hour she would have lived. The deep satisfaction which her being demands would travel through those exacerbated centres of speech, and we should have quiet.'

It was always difficult to know how much the doctor meant what he said and when he was having a joke at your expense. The captain's blue eyes, however, twinkled mischievously.

'Well, Doctor, I have great confidence in your powers of diagnosis. The remedy you suggest is evidently worth trying, and since you are a bachelor it is clear that it is up to you to apply it.'

'Pardon me, Captain, it is my professional duty to prescribe remedies for the patients under my charge in this ship, but not to administer them personally. Besides, I am sixty.'

'I am a married man with grown-up children,' said the captain. 'I am old and fat and asthmatic, it is obvious that I cannot be expected to undertake a task of this kind. Nature cut me out for the role of husband and father, not for that of a lover.'

'Youth in these matters is essential and good looks are advantageous,' said the doctor gravely.

The captain gave a great bang on the table with his fist.

'You are thinking of Hans. You're quite right. Hans must do it.'

The mate sprang to his feet.

'Me? Never.'

'Hans, you are tall, handsome, strong as a lion, brave and young. We have twenty-three days more at sea before we reach Hamburg, you wouldn't desert your trusted old captain in an emergency or let down your good friend the doctor?'

'No, Captain, it's asking too much of me. I have been married less than a year and I love my wife. I can hardly wait to get back to Hamburg. She is yearning for me as I am yearning for her. I will not be unfaithful to her, especially with Miss Reid.'

'Miss Reid's not so bad,' said the doctor.

'Some people might call her even nice-looking,' said the

captain.

And indeed when you took Miss Reid feature by feature she was not in fact a plain woman. True, she had a long, stupid face, but her brown eyes were large and she had very thick lashes; her brown hair was cut short and curled rather prettily over her neck; she hadn't a bad skin, and she was neither too fat nor too thin. She was not old as people go nowadays, and if she had told you that she was forty you would have been quite willing to believe it. The only thing against her was that she was drab and dull.

'Must I then for twenty-three mortal days endure the prolixity of that tedious woman? Must I for twenty-three mortal days answer her inane questions and listen to her fatuous remarks? Must I, an old man, have my Sylvester Abend, the jolly evening I was looking forward to, ruined by the unwelcome company of that intolerable virgin? And all because no one can be found to show a little gallantry, a little human kindness, a spark of charity to a lonely woman. I shall wreck the ship.'

'There's always the radio-operator,' said Hans.

The captain gave a loud shout.

'Hans, let the ten thousand virgins of Cologne arise and call you blessed. Steward,' he bellowed, 'tell the radio-operator that I want him.'

The radio-operator came into the saloon and smartly clicked his heels together. The three men looked at him in silence. He wondered uneasily whether he had done something for which he was about to be hauled over the coals. He was above the middle height, with square shoulders and narrow hips, erect and slender, his tanned, smooth skin looked as though a razor had never touched it, he had large eyes of a startling blue and a mane of curling golden hair. He was a perfect specimen of young Teutonic manhood. He was so healthy, so vigorous, so much alive that even when he stood some way from you, you felt the glow of his vitality.

'Aryan, all right,' said the captain. 'No doubt about that. How old are you, my boy?'

'Twenty-one, sir.'

'Married?'

'No, sir.'

'Engaged?'

The radio-operator chuckled. There was an engaging boyishness in his laugh.

'No, sir.'

'You know we have a female passenger on board?'

'Yes, sir.'

'Do you know her?'

'I've said good morning to her when I've seen her on deck.'

The captain assumed his most official manner. His eyes, which generally twinkled with fun, were stern and he got a sort of bark into his rich, fruity voice.

'Although this is a cargo-boat and we carry valuable freight, we also take such passengers as we can get, and this is a branch of our business that the company is anxious to encourage. My instructions are to do everything possible to promote the happiness and comfort of the passengers. Miss Reid needs a lover. The doctor and I have come to the conclusion that you are well suited to satisfy Miss Reid's requirements.'

'Me, sir?'

The radio-operator blushed scarlet and then began to giggle, but quickly composed himself when he saw the set faces of the three men who confronted him.

'But she's old enough to be my mother.'

'That at your age is a matter of no consequence. She is a woman of the highest distinction and allied to all the great families of England. If she were German she would be at least a countess. That you should have been chosen for this responsible position is an honour that you should greatly appreciate. Furthermore, your English is halting and this will give you an excellent opportunity to improve it.'

'That of course is something to be thought of,' said the radio-operator. 'I know that I want practice.'

'It is not often in this life that it is possible to combine pleasure with intellectual improvement, and you must congratulate yourself on your good fortune.'

'But if I may be allowed to put the question, sir, why does Miss Reid want a lover?'

'It appears to be an old English custom for unmarried women of exalted rank to submit themselves to the embraces of a lover at this time of year. The company is anxious that Miss Reid should be treated exactly as she would be on an English ship, and we trust that if she is satisfied, with her aristocratic connections she will be able to persuade many of her friends to take cruises in the line's ships.'

'Sir, I must ask to be excused.'

'It is not a request I am making, it is an order. You will present yourself to Miss Reid, in her cabin, at eleven o'clock tonight.'

'What shall I do when I get there?'

'Do?' thundered the captain. 'Do? Act naturally.'

With a wave of the hand he dismissed him. The radio-operator clicked his heels, saluted and went out.

'Now let us have another glass of beer,' said the captain.

At supper that evening Miss Reid was at her best. She was verbose. She was playful. She was refined. There was not a truism that she failed to utter. There was not a commonplace that she forebore to express. She bombarded them with foolish questions. The captain's face grew redder and redder as he sought to contain his fury; he felt that he could not go on being polite to her any longer and if the doctor's remedy did not help, one day he would forget himself and give her, not a piece, but the whole of his mind.

'I shall lose my job,' he thought, 'but I'm not sure that it wouldn't be worth it.'

Next day they were already sitting at table when she came in to dinner.

'Sylvester Abend tomorrow,' she said brightly. That was the sort of thing she would say. She went on: 'Well, what have you all been up to this morning?'

Since they did exactly the same thing every day, and she knew very well what that was, the question was enraging. The Captain's heart sank. He briefly told the doctor what he thought of him.

'Now, no German, please,' said Miss Reid archly. 'You know I don't allow that, and why, Captain, did you give the poor doctor that sour look? It's Christmas time, you know; peace and good-will to all men. I'm so excited about tomorrow evening, and will there be candles on the Christmas tree?'

'Naturally.'

'How thrilling! I always think a Christmas tree without candles isn't a Christmas tree. Oh, d'you know, I had such a funny experience last night. I can't understand it at all.'

A startled pause. They all looked intently at Miss Reid. For once they hung on her lips.

'Yes,' she went on in that monotonous, rather finicking way of hers, 'I was just getting into bed last night when there was a knock at my door. "Who is it?" I said. "It's the radio-operator," was the answer. "What is it?" I said. "Can I speak to you?" he said.'

They listened with rapt attention.

' "Well, I'll just pop on a dressing-gown," I said, "and open the door." So I popped on a dressing-gown and opened the door. The radio-operator said: "Excuse me, miss, but do you want to send a radio?" Well, I did think it was funny his coming at that hour to ask me if I wanted to send a radio, I just laughed in his face, it appealed to my sense of humour if you understand what I mean, but I didn't want to hurt his feelings so I said: "Thank you so much, but I don't think I want to send a radio". He stood there, looking so funny, as if he was quite embarrassed, so I said: "Thank you all the same for asking me," and then I said "Good night, pleasant dreams" and shut the door.'

'The damned fool,' cried the captain.

'He's young, Miss Reid,' the doctor put in. 'It was excess of zeal. I suppose he thought you would want to send a New Year's greeting to your friends and he wished you to get the advantage of the special rate.'

'Oh, I didn't mind at all. I like these queer little things that happen to one when one's travelling. I just get a good laugh out of them.'

As soon as dinner was over and Miss Reid had left them the captain sent for the radio-operator.

'You idiot, what in heaven's name made you ask Miss Reid last night whether she wanted to send a radio?'

'Sir, you told me to act naturally. I am a radio-operator. I though it natural to ask her if she wanted to send a radio. I didn't know what else to say.'

'God in heaven,' shouted the captain, 'when Siegfried saw Brünhilde lying on her rock and cried: *Das ist kein Mann,*' (the captain sang the words, and being pleased with the sound of his voice, repeated the phrase two or three times before he continued), 'did Siegfried when she awoke ask her if she wished to send a radio, to announce to her papa, I suppose, that she was sitting up after her long sleep and taking notice?'

'I beg most respectfully to draw your attention to the fact that Brünhilde was Siegfried's aunt. Miss Reid is a total stranger to me.'

'He did not reflect that she was his aunt. He knew only that she was a beautiful and defenceless woman of obviously good family and he acted as any gentleman would have done. You are young, handsome, Aryan to the tips of your fingers, the honour of Germany is in your hands.'

'Very good, sir. I will do my best.'

That night there was another knock on Miss Reid's door.

'Who is it?'

'The radio-operator. I have a radio for you, Miss Reid.'

'For me.' She was surprised, but it at once occurred to her that one of her fellow passengers who had got off at Haiti had sent her New Year's greetings. 'How very kind people are,' she thought. 'I'm in bed. Leave it outside the door.'

'It needs an answer. Ten words prepaid.'

Then it couldn't be a New Year's greeting. Her heart stopped beating. It could only mean one thing; her shop had been burned to the ground. She jumped out of bed.

'Slip it under the door and I'll write the answer and slip it back to you.'

The envelope was pushed under the door and as it appeared on the carpet it had really a sinister look. Miss Reid snatched it up and tore the envelope open. The words swam before her eyes and she couldn't for a moment find her spectacles. This is what she read:

'Happy New Year. Stop. Peace and goodwill to all men. Stop. You are very beautiful. Stop. I love you. Stop. I must speak to you. Stop. Signed: Radio Operator.'

Miss Reid read this through twice. Then she slowly took off her spectacles and hid them under a scarf. She opened the door.

'Come in,' she said.

Next day was New Year's Eve. The officers were cheerful and a little sentimental when they sat down to dinner. The stewards had decorated the saloon with tropical creepers to make up for

holly and mistletoe, and the Christmas tree stood on a table with
the candles ready to be lit at supper time. Miss Reid did not come
in till the officers were seated, and when they bade her good
morning she did not speak but merely bowed. They looked at her
curiously. She ate a good dinner, but uttered never a word. Her
silence was uncanny. At last the captain could stand it no
longer, and he said:

'You're very quiet today, Miss Reid.'

'I'm thinking,' she remarked.

'And will you tell us your thoughts, Miss Reid?' the doctor
asked playfully.

She gave him a cool, you might almost have called it a super-
cilious look.

'I prefer to keep them to myself, Doctor. I will have a little
more of that hash, I've got a very good appetite.'

They finished the meal in a blessed silence. The captain heaved
a sigh of relief. That was what meal-time was for, to eat, not to
chatter. When they had finished he went up to doctor and wrung
his hand.

'Something has happened, Doctor.'

'It has happened. She's a changed woman.'

'But will it last?'

'One can only hope for the best.'

Miss Reid put on an evening dress for the evening's celebration, a very quiet black dress, with artifical roses at her bosom
and a long string of imitation jade round her neck. The lights
were dimmed and the candles on the Christmas tree were lit. It
felt a little like being in church. The junior officers were supping
in the saloon that evening and they looked very smart in their
white uniforms. Champagne was served at the company's expense
and after supper they had a *Maibowle**. They pulled crackers.
They sang songs to the gramophone, *Deutschland, Deutschland
über Alles, Alt Heidelberg* and *Auld Lang Syne*. They shouted
out the tunes lustily, the captain's voice rising loud above the
others, and Miss Reid joining in with a pleasing contralto. The
doctor noticed that Miss Reid's eyes from time to time rested on
the radio-operator, and in them he read an expression of some

*Bowl of may-wine, wine and champagne flavoured with herbs.

bewilderment.

'He's a good-looking fellow, isn't he?' said the doctor.

Miss Reid turned round and looked at the doctor coolly.

'Who?'

'The radio-operator. I thought you were looking at him.'

'Which is he?'

'The duplicity of women,' the doctor muttered, but with a smile he answered: 'He's sitting next to the chief engineer.'

'Oh, of course, I recognise him now. You know, I never think it matters what a man looks like. I'm so much more interested in a man's brains than in his looks.'

'Ah,' said the doctor.

They all got a little tight, including Miss Reid, but she did not lose her dignity and when she bade them good-night it was in her best manner.

'I've had a very delightful evening. I shall never forget my New Year's Eve on a German boat. It's been very interesting. Quite an experience.'

She walked steadily to the door, and this was something of a triumph, for she had drunk drink for drink with the rest of them through the evening.

They were all somewhat jaded next day. When the captain, the mate, the doctor and the chief engineer came down to dinner they found Miss Reid already seated. Before each place was a small parcel tied up in pink ribbon. On each was written: Happy New Year. They gave Miss Reid a questioning glance.

'You've all been so very kind to me I thought I'd like to give each of you a little present. There wasn't much choice at Port au Prince, so you mustn't expect too much.'

There was pair of briar pipes for the captain, half a dozen silk handkerchiefs for the doctor, a cigar-case for the mate and a couple of ties for the chief engineer. They had dinner and Miss Reid retired to her cabin to rest. The officers looked at one another uncomfortably. The mate fiddled with the cigar case she had given him.

'I'm a little ashamed of myself,' he said at last.

The captain was pensive and it was plain that he too was a trifle uneasy.

'I wonder if we ought to have played that trick on Miss

Reid,' he said. 'She's a good old soul and she's not rich; she's a woman who earns her own living. She must have spent the best part of a hundred marks on these presents. I almost wish we'd left her alone.'

The doctor shrugged his shoulders.

'You wanted her silenced and I've silenced her.'

'When all's said and done, it wouldn't have hurt us to listen to her chatter for three weeks more,' said the mate.

'I'm not happy about her,' added the captain. 'I feel there's something ominous in her quietness.'

She had spoken hardly a word during the meal they had just shared with her. She seemed hardly to listen to what they said.

'Don't you think you ought to ask her if she's feeling quite well, doctor?' suggested the captain.

'Of course she's feeling quite well. She's eating like a wolf. If you want inquiries made you'd much better make them of the radio-operator.'

'You may not be aware of it, Doctor, but I am a man of great delicacy.'

'I am a man of heart myself,' said the doctor.

For the rest of the journey those men spoilt Miss Reid outrageously. They treated her with with the consideration they would have shown to someone who was convalescent after a long and dangerous illness. Though her appetite was excellent they sought to tempt her with new dishes. The doctor ordered wine and insisted on her sharing his bottle with him. They played dominoes with her. They played chess with her. They played bridge with her. They engaged her in conversation. But there was no doubt about it, though she responded to their advances with politeness, she kept herself to herself. She seemed to regard them with something very like disdain; you might almost have thought that she looked upon those men and their efforts to be amiable as pleasantly ridiculous. She seldom spoke unless spoken to. She read detective stories and at night sat on deck looking at the stars. She lived a life of her own.

At last the journey drew to its close. They sailed up the English Channel on a still grey day; they sighted land. Miss Reid packed her trunk. At two o'clock in the afternoon they docked at Plymouth. The captain, the mate and the doctor came along to say good-bye to her.

'Well, Miss Reid,' said the captain in his jovial way, 'we're sorry to lose you, but I suppose you're glad to be getting home.'

'You've been very kind to me, you've all been very kind to me, I don't know what I've done to deserve it. I've been very happy with you. I shall never forget you.'

She spoke rather shakily, she tried to smile, but her lips quivered, and tears ran down her cheeks. The captain got very red. He smiled awkwardly.

'May I kiss you, Miss Reid?'

She was taller than he by half a head. She bent down and he planted a fat kiss on one wet cheek and a fat kiss on the other. She turned to the mate and the doctor. They both kissed her.

'What an old fool I am,' she said. 'Everybody's so good.'

She dried her eyes and slowly, in her graceful, rather absurd way, walked down the companion. The captain's eyes were wet. When she reached the quay she looked up and waved to someone on the boat deck.

'Who's she waving to?' asked the captain.

'The radio-operator.'

Miss Price was waiting on the quay to welcome her. When they had passed the customs and got rid of Miss Reid's heavy luggage they went to Miss Price's house and had an early cup of tea. Miss Reid's train did not start till five. Miss Price had much to tell Miss Reid.

'But it's too bad of me to go on like this when you've just come home. I've been looking forward to hearing all about your journey.'

'I'm afraid there's not very much to tell.'

'I can't believe that. Your trip was a success, wasn't it?'

'A distinct success. It was very nice.'

'And you didn't mind being with all those Germans?'

'Of course they're not like English people. One has to get used to their ways. They sometimes do things that—well, that English people wouldn't do, you know. But I always think that one has to take things as they come.'

'What sort of things do you mean?'

Miss Reid looked at her friend calmly. Her long, stupid face had a placid look, and Miss Price never noticed that in the eyes was a strangely mischievous twinkle.

'Things of no importance really. Just funny, unexpected, rather nice things. There's no doubt that travel is a wonderful education.'

Suggestions for further reading

Apart from the juvenile *Orientations* (1899) and one volume published posthumously, Maugham's stories were often first published in magazines and were then arranged in eight volumes between 1921 and 1947. They have since been collected and arranged by the author in four volumes which are available in paperback. *The Trembling of a Leaf* (1921) and *The Casuarina Tree* (1926), which deal with the difficulties of expatriate life in remote colonies, first established Maugham as a popular story-writer.

Maugham's first novel *Liza of Lambeth* is really a long short story dealing with the life, love and death of Liza in the East End of London. Even today it is still harrowing in its realism as well as having acquired appeal as a period-piece. Also recommended are: *Of Human Bondage* (1915), a long and partly autobiographical novel dealing with the trials of youth and young manhood of Philip Carey; *The Moon and Sixpence* (1919), a colourful tale of the life of Charles Strickland (based on Paul Gauguin), who abandons the security of his family and position as a stockbroker for the life of a painter in Paris and Tahiti; and *Cakes and Ale* (1930) which exposes the literary world which Maugham knew in London and which is now famous for the character of Rosie.

Information about the author's life and opinions is to be found in *The Summing Up* (1938), *A Writer's Notebook* (1949), and the *Prefaces* to the novels. The student of the short story will also find Maugham's essay on the subject in *Points of View* (1958) of interest.

William Sansom (1912-1976)

In 1941 the novelist and short story-writer H. E. Bates predicted that the widening of experience for all kinds of people caused by the Second World War would produce a good crop of short stories. William Sansom's career provides an example of what H. E. Bates expected to happen on a much larger scale.

Sansom had worked in a bank, as an advertising copywriter, as a pianist and composer, as a radio script-writer and had submitted large numbers of formula magazine stories to editors and publishers. None was accepted. However, between shifts as a London fireman during the Blitz he described his experiences and the first of these pieces, entitled *The Wall*, was published almost by accident in the magazine *Horizon*. The success of this and other stories encouraged him to give up his job and become a full-time writer in 1945. The first and most difficult lesson had been learned, as Sansom himself recalls: 'No story is new, only its ingredients; and those ingredients had best be taken from life, not books. The writer must be observer and public detective.' The Society of Authors awarded him a travelling scholarship in 1946 and this opportunity to travel in order to write accounts for the volume *South— Aspects and Images from Corsica, Italy and Southern France,* from which *My Little Robins* is taken. It will probably come as no surprise to learn that Sansom was a keen, if amateur, painter. Thus the eye of the professional writer combined with that of the amateur painter to produce the splendid descriptive writing, with its exact handling of detail and sensitive awareness of the changing moods of weather, which is one of the hallmarks of Sansom's writing.

Another lesson which Sansom learnt very early on was the value of economy. As a copywriter he had seen advertisements reduced several times to fit new columns and smaller budgets. They emerged apparently unscathed, often with an extra succinctness. This was later confirmed by a writer friend who ruthlessly pruned away all the words in a piece which were not essential. Such economy is fundamental to the short story. One of the reasons the reader's interest is maintained at such a consistently high level in Sansom's work is that there are no fallow areas. Every detail counts. The recollections within Mr Bowlsend's monologue (in *The Day the Lift . . .*); the speed at which he approaches the lift; the most grotesque of Rodney's economies (in *Where Liberty Lies*): none of these ingredients can be skipped without losing important information. Sansom's natural love of words is kept strictly in check and this restraint proves to be an excellent stimulus.

Sansom is a craftsman in prose but this is not solely an intellectual activity. 'When writing a story I like to see that all the senses are involved, sound, sight, smell, touch, taste plus such ancillary divisions as colour and, where apposite, a reference to an evocative piece of music.' Sensation, particularly tactile and aural, is always present in the stories. Look for instance at the unerring facility with which Sansom handles dialogue, the subtle nuances of conversation which tell so much more than is actually spoken.

Two further characteristics of Sansom's stories deserve particular mention. The first is his ability to create suspense, to set up a tension between the reader and the protagonist(s) which is not broken until the close of the story or the dénouement where this is employed. Sometimes we are given an obvious hint, as with the Corsican engineer: 'There was nothing odd in what he did though later it was to prove otherwise.' Even without this the man's dynamism is such that we, like Sansom, would be compelled to follow the blue képi around Ajaccio. In *The Day The Lift . . .* the tension is to some extent created by the situation, as with a similar incident in *No Smoking on the Apron,* but we are still anxious to find out how the capable and orderly Arnold Brinsley will finally cope with his ordeal. This is one aspect of Sansom's technique which may not appeal to all readers and it is certainly less effective when applied to the expanded novel form. The final quality is one for which above everything else Sansom will continue to be read: his ability to poke fun at his characters which is inextricably bound up with his tender love for his fellow beings, 'the load of lovely human litter' who fill the bar in *Eventide* for instance. It is difficult to imagine more contrasting Londoners than Arnold Brinsley Bowlsend and Rodney and yet the two men are described with delicate irony and a humour which is both objective and sympathetic.

Many of Sansom's stories originally appeared in the literary periodicals of the time, e.g. *Horizon, The Cornhill, Penguin New Writing, English*

Story, London Magazine and *Argosy,* and three collections were published before his first novel *The Body.* It is principally through the stories that his reputation has become established. *The Body* shares its theme with an early story *Through the Quinquina Glass* (which incidentally gives a valuable insight into the process of composition), and I leave the reader to decide which he finds most successful. There seems little doubt, however, that Sansom's very considerable gifts as a writer find their best expression through the medium of the short story, of which the following examples represent a delightful but all too brief selection.

My Little Robins

That notable engineer first made his appearance one night on the Ligurian Sea, on the Ajaccio passage.

At nine or ten o'clock I was sitting huddled in a corner of the second-class saloon. One heavily shaded light burned above a flap-table that served, with its four or five bottles, as a bar. The rest of the saloon faded off on all sides into darkness, the darkness of bulwark-shaped walls and a portholed fore-partition: in the darkness lay passengers in all the humped and sprawled positions of shipboard sleep. They lay among the litter of their suppers—bread-rind, cheese-crumbs, wine bottles—and the crumpled shreds of newspaper in which all that food had been wrapped; among the first pale reachings of vomit; against shoulders and on laps, on Corsicans sailing back to their native island, on Corsican nieces visiting their old aunts in mountain villages, on Corsican entrepreneurs of Ajaccio, on the sons of Corsicans returning from their universities in France, on Corsican travellers in chestnuts and granite and wood, on long-moustached migrants homing again, on matriarchs intent upon the hearths of their first brooding—on all these who were bound together by the second-class look, dark and roughish, bound with the wicker-basket and the peasant spattering that distinguish both ships bound for islands and ships of the inland seas, rough ships that ply the Black Sea, the Caspian, the local Baltic and this the Ligurian Sea bound for Ajaccio in French Corsica.

And now into the sleep-smelling saloon, shuddering from the engines aft, dusky with the cramp of travellers, there stepped the bright-blue dungarees of an engineer. He entered firmly, straight from his engines, with a seaman's tread; stood for a moment wiping some of the oil from his hands; stepped over to the circle of light over the makeshift bar. Disregarding the passengers, he fingered a packet of cigarettes from his dungaree pockets, held it high to drop a cigarette unsoiled into his mouth, then ordered a pastis. He held the milky glass outstretched, curling out one long finger in a gesture of stiff delicacy—and drank. This man's presence was forceful—instantly one was affected. There was nothing odd in what he did—though later it was to prove otherwise. The appearance in the second-class saloon of a ship's worker, an ordinary engineer, was not unusual to any but a few northern passengers accustomed to firmer disciplinary divisions on larger and colder ships. It was more his personal figure; and, of course, some essential power beneath this.

He did not look like what an engineer might be supposed to look. He was a tall, thin, gangling man, with a beaked nose and dark bright eyes that peered forward with the look of any angry scholar. His thin stomach arched in, his knees knobbled and bent forward, his arms held bonily akimbo, he moved—and he moved all the time, he never stopped—like an agitated don doing his best with a fox-trot. Often the scholarly, the nominally un-worldly, lurch and stumble not so much because their bodies have been misshapen by the length of their books, as by a deficiency in ordinary vanity—they have never worshipped bodily grace in a manner personal enough to imitate it; they are neither nervous nor preoccupied, simply they have never learned. But this is often compensated by a delicacy of smaller movements—gestures of the hands, inclinations of the head, reclinations of the whole body. Thus also the engineer: his hands, long-fingered, black-oiled, fluttered beautifully; the movements of his head followed fluently the thoughts of his mind, and even standing his whole body was sitting—he drooped relaxed. He wore dark sunglasses, and perched on his head a blue cap crumpled like a képi* from the Crimean war.

He never stopped moving. As he took his glass and first sur-veyed it, he arched further backwards, and then as he drank re-volved slowly with his lips to the glass, scrutinising the deep half-circle of sleepers; simultaneously he managed to speak to the bar-

*French military cap with a horizontal peak.

man and wave with his free hand to one of the passengers who was still sitting upright and awake. Now taking his drink he gangled over to this man, and started an intense gesticulated conversation. His body swayed, his hands fluttered, his nose pecked, his eyes rolled. He spoke in French in either a Provençal or Italian dialect. It was difficult to understand all he said—but it had to do with prices, the loan of a gun, and the sale of something he had brought from the mainland. It was plain now that some of his volatility was moved by the common Mediterranean need for commerce, for using each moment as a street-corner; yet this too he managed with a curious distinction. The other man said little, sometimes shrugged his shoulders—his was the situation of the approached. But finally, as if forces had been slowly gathering inside him, he too began to talk, without pause, giving with definition his own idea of the matter; he pointed suddenly to his stomach, and began to talk faster and louder. The engineer opened his arms wide, and managed at the same time to move his shoulders up and down in a series of hopeless shrugs. Impossible, the shoulders said, hopeless. The other man drew from his pocket a note—twenty francs. The shrugging ceased, the engineer took the note—though indeed still as if there could be no hope, with down-pressed lips that expressed also something of the worthlessness of all money—and went shuffling and lurching from the saloon. In a few moments he returned, carrying bread and a huge dish of soup. The man nodded and began to eat. Just then, I suppose, my eyes closed and I was off to sleep.

I was to see much of this engineer, but I did not catch sight of him again until quite late the next morning.

We put into Ajaccio early—at dawn. The great U-shaped gulf, long enough to contain two thousand ships, received us with grey swelling waters, while on either side the black mountainous coast-line raced out to sea; the first pink light burnt its foundry-glare into a chilled grey sky, a red glow had already painted the curious Iles Sanguinaires with the wet of new blood. Those three sinister islands stood off the cape in a line that seemed to move. Well inside lay Ajaccio and its few sprouting palms.

Even at that distance the town, huddled down low against the dark mountains, looked poor and squalid. And then, as we neared its long façade, and the ship seemed to fly through the water with each flat square-windowed building marking its speed, that grey light showed clearly the scabrous texture of each wall, the cracked and peeling and stained surface of decay. Later, when the sun had risen and I was warming over a glass of coffee on the Cours Napoléon, the sun threw into sharper definition the ulcerous scars, the gutter-soaked patches that smeared the walls of all those tall barrack-like buildings. The kerbs had fallen away, sand from the pavements had run in rivulets out on to the pocked carriageway of this the main street of the capital; no soft grasses and lichens pursued such decay, but instead only sand and powdered asphalt giving with their dull ochreous aridity the tone of the town, a town of huge barrack-buildings, dry palms and now leafless plane-trees, of Senegalese troops and occasional statues of Napoléon, of garbage in the streets and a wide main square of sand, of sand and the tricolour. Two main avenues converged on that immense sandy Place Diamant; along one, the Cours Napoléon, men in many clothes were already sipping their pastis and talking.

I was to know later that in these lines of cafés and bars there was no dancing, only pastis and cards—this was much a garrison town, a port for sailors and land-locked soldiers, upon which one could feel written in the sand and round the monuments and over the acres of blighted plaster the hideous word 'caserne'.

Suddenly I saw again my engineer. He was dressed as before—pale-blue overalls, képi, black glasses; he was thus sharply visible among the khakis and corduroys and greys of the growing crowd. He came gesturing and gangling from the dark door of a bar, as fast as if he had been ejected, holding under one arm a package and in the other the arm of a much shorter and fatter man whom he now dragged at speed along the street. Both men talked fast and without pause, even in their linked position managing to turn their faces close and vehement. They disappeared down one of the steep side streets to the Rue Cardinal Fesch.

Having nothing particular to do but look at the town, I rose and followed. They had chosen this little street for a transaction, and now stood, still gesturing and exploding, between a foot-high mass of cabbage and dung and one of the leaning house-walls with its fat china drainpipe. Then, at some climax, the engineer flourished his parcel, tore off the brown paper, and stood for a moment without talking, his wide black glasses staring wonderstruck at the beauty of what was revealed—an American army jacket and breeches. The smaller man showed instant disgust, looked up and down the street for something, anything amusing. But at the same time his left hand fingered the material of the jacket. The engineer was talking again. The small man kept shrugging his shoulders. At last, with the down-drawn lips and heavenward eyes of a dying martyr, he shuffled in his pocket and brought out some notes. He took the clothes, handed the engineer the notes. A pause. Then the blue form of the engineer exploded. He rose on his toes, bending over the other man like a furious bird, hands wide outstretched like eagle's wings, his nose-beaked head pecking forward with every emphatic word. The smaller man parried this by staring up at him with his head on one side, a small smile of unbelief cocking the corner of his mouth—a sceptic child surveyed his hysterical uncle. But the volcano proved too much, its force grew until the smile disappeared. A last shrug of his shoulders. Then reaching into a pocket that small man drew forth a handful of red cylinders. Cartridges. And these instantly the engineer took, hiding them, subsiding and simultaneously throwing a hand of affection on his adversary's shoulder. They then parted on the best, on the face of it, of terms.

The engineer walked quickly up into the main street again and disappeared into a bar. I stood waiting for him to come out—fascinated by such volatility, by such an exquisite performance of the Mediterranean pantomime of buy-sell, where the marks of pity and contempt, ennui and obsession, despair and joy, are seen publicly at their finest extremes. That concession to the blind eye of the police when one moves off the main street yet deals in the open! The etiquette of silence while the other talks! That entrance at a predetermined point of the score into inspired duet . . . but now the engineer came bursting out from the bar with a shotgun under his arm. This altered his manner absolutely, the shotgun slaughtered innocence. With his dark glasses glazing obsessedly ahead, he strode off to the Place Diamant, whose circuit he made, keeping to the wall.

Along past the dark yellow military hospital, down the sea-wall with its row of stunted palms like elephant legs tufted wearily with green feathers. Along the road that skirts the side of the gulf, a road marked by a gradual scarcity of building, a greater decrepitude in the roadway, by refuse dumps and isolated half-finished concrete tenements, by bones and offal and driftwood lying puddled in the red rockpools: and always by the attempt of public work to be worthy of a capital, but an attempt forlorn, abandoned at its start, as though some tremendous force of nature had weighed too heavily down on the hopeless community of human hearts. A weight of nature was implemented—for now to either side the majesty of this island of mountains began to impress itself. Those mountains on the far side of the gulf raced their black humps far into the sea, snow on their peaks glittered like sugar in the sun, pockets of poisonous wool drifted longingly across the valley cuts; while to the right of our road rose the near slopes of the maquis, small ascending mountains thickly covered with aromatic scrub, so that they looked smooth and furry, like convulsed green baize.

The engineer walked fast, bouncing on his toes, throwing his elbows back and jolting like a professional walker. His head under that képi now searched the terrain to the right: he might have been looking for one of the few scattered villas that straggled about the slope. On he went. We passed a sudden, then endless cemetery of bright stone house-tombs, each built much more stably than the houses back in the capital—sealed evidences of Corsican pride and familiarity with death. Abruptly the cemetery ceased and the road grew houseless and wild, with no embankment against the gulf, and growing on either side wet green cactus studded with yellow flowers. The Iles Sanguinaires moved like a line of ships in the distance. The maquis rose un-walled on our right.

The engineer stopped, glanced keenly up the hillside. Very quickly he took cartridges from his pocket—I saw them flash red as they were snapped away into the gun. Then he was off climb-ing up the steep, rough incline. He climbed like a frog, spreading his hands and long thin legs to grasp branches and to grip the greyish boulders, thrusting forward his body against the gradient. It was hardly prudent to follow him immediately—on a road my presence might have been coincidental, but on the pathless maquis not. I waited.

In fact, was it prudent to follow him at all? There he went, purposely armed, intent on some firm direction—probably some goat-herd's shack, some outlying cottage. The morning paper had already told me that the day before, yesterday, there had been a shooting in the main café in Ajaccio—a husband seated with his wife and another man had suddenly risen to his feet and shot this other man bluntly in the stomach. And some time in the recent past a night-club manager had shot a sailor in the neck for disturbing his orchestra with an impromptu on the accordion. There had been bullet holes in the mirror of another café. And the Corsican is renowned for his history of proud summary justice. Whatever then the engineer would do might involve me, if I remained so close—either as an accomplice, or as a witness. Or the engineer himself would shoot me as a spy? However . . . the affair was too mature to abandon. Besides, we were in the country, with no easy diversions. So I decided to climb up into the maquis at a parallel distance from the engineer, to climb faster and thus higher than him, so that I could look down on his direction. With the cover afforded by scrub it would be fairly simple to remain unobserved—and my suit was grey, where his was bright-washed blue.

A sweaty climb under the rising sun. The maquis is a strange mixture of hard and soft things, of sudden aromatic carpets of herb, of eruptions of hard grey boulders, of soft arbutus and cystus, and then of spiny cactus. But mostly it feels soft, looking so moss-green, the hill-top a high ridge of green fur against the blue sky; the air smells sweet as so many odorous plants are crushed by the heel. Though it was steep and tiring, the climb was a joy; a sense of great freedom among such windwashed luxuriance in the warm winter sun made me forget the engineer. Or postpone him. But arrived at last at my eminence I took cover, and looked round. He was nowhere to be seen. I felt in my haversack for the glasses, and then began to scrutinise carefully the intricate shrub.

No sound. No movement over all the expanse of rolling lichenous sward—only sometimes the silent glint of a bird skimming the low branches, or curving up suddenly like a feather kicked on hot air. The arm of scented green stretched out to sea

—for this was the thick upper arm of a cape—and on either side extended, far and near, the sea. No forest murmur here, no trees to move in those slight breezes that fanned the two shores: it was deadly set, like a painted plaster model. In ancient times pilots knew this island from a distance because of the perfume that drifted far out over the sea, a perfume of flowering scrub that caused those ancient oarsmen to call it the Scented Isle. But now it was winter, warm but flowerless—and still.

The black sockets of my binoculars traversed slowly. Up the slight hills, down suddenly into the overgrown ravines, past a ruined goatherd's hut, over a circle of stones that had once based a sheep-pen or a Genoese watch-tower. Suddenly I saw the peaked blue képi, a pale-blue tropical bird above a bush of myrtle. The man was crouched, moving sideways with the gun stealthily creeping to his shoulder. The dark glasses were fixed emotionless and ruthless on something at the centre of a circle he was making; my glasses were focused clear on those dark others. A slow movement, trying to make no sound—and in the binoculars there was an augmented silence. Over all, the immense quiet of the day.

It was difficult to move the binoculars off him. At such a moment he might have made some decisive move, disappearing into the bush. But at length, as his movements seemed to remain so steady, I shifted those back circles carefully across. There was nothing.

I searched in vain—for a hut, for some other man's movement, for the movement of a branch that might show up some other man. But there was nothing—and I knew by the direction of his glasses that he was anticipating no long shot. Whoever he was after lay close. No movement, no life in that scrub—only suddenly a pinpoint of colour that intensified the strange still-ness. A robin sat on one of the branches. Its orange breast caught the sunlight, it was opening and shutting its beak as if trying to sing—for of course no sound came.

It did not seem possible. At first I discarded the idea. But as the minutes passed the truth emerged; irrefutable and, through the glasses, of strange isolated power. The engineer was stalking that robin. I switched the glasses to and fro, certainly the gun's barrel was trained on the little bird's level. But—why not shoot?

Then, as the engineer quietly lowered his head to the gunsight, it was plain to see why he held his fire. He had been moving round *behind the robin*. Some deep amazing instinct had instructed him to shoot this little bird in the back.

For a long time the scene stayed fixed. The man's head was now lowered to the sights, so that the peak of his pale képi ran parallel with the gun. It looked more than ever like a bird, or like some false effigy of a bird, a pointed blue-beaked thing like a carnival mask, like the cruel disguise of some grotesque bird-watcher's hood. And a few yards across the scented foliage, whose every fragile leaf was set so still, there sat the other bird, the real little bird. With its back turned. So that the two made a silent unmoving procession of birds. Not a leaf shivered; they were like leaves seen on a cinema film, bright and unreal. The figure in the képi seemed cast in wax. Only the little bird's mouth could be seen faintly moving—perhaps eating. That small movement only accentuated the silence, as though the bird were singing without sound.

Suddenly it rose in the air, blasted by a sudden wind, and then with scattering wings dropped. At the same time the foliage behind shivered. Then a drift of smoke came, and a prancing blue figure—just as the echoing shot-sound cracked as if behind my ear. I kept the binoculars fixed, my two holes of vision showed the blue figure thrashing excitedly in the tangled shrub, eagerly pounding then lifting aloft, with a backward-leaning motion of triumph, a small furry ball of grey and orange.

Some hours later, having lunched in Ajaccio, I saw him again. He was talking to elderly Corsicans. He held in his hand a small bunch of little birds—three at least were robins. These he brandished in the faces of the two old men, who seemed annoyed and looked pointedly away. This time I determined to hear what was said. They were standing at a point that I could approach without seeming inquisitive.

They were standing near to the old fountain in the barrack wall. Here, in a stone recess behind an iron railing, was a place where old men habitually forgathered. Such old men stood there for hours, leaning on the iron railing, gossiping, gazing at the passers-by of the Place Diamant and past them across the

sandy waste to the leprous line of houses stretching to the gulf-
wall, at the gulf and its sombre mountains beyond. The engineer
and his two acquaintances were standing outside the railing. It
seemed that only the poorer went inside, men who had had their
day; and somehow they must have formed a focal point for street
standing, because it was around here that a ragged crowd always
loitered and talked. This I now joined.

After a few hours on the island my understanding of the patois
was growing clearer. They spoke Corsican—not the romance language of the midi, but a mixture of French and Genoese. The
two old men were pure islanders. They wore the wide curl-
brimmed black hats, the long jackets of chestnut brown corduroy, the bright-scarlet cummerbunds that still form a much-
worn national dress among the older country-people. And Ajaccio,
besides being a caserne, still retained some of the feeling of a large
market town, it attracted people from the hills, the farmers, the
millers, the sons of labourers and gentlemen and bandits. These
old two, with their lean high cheekbones and their draped mous-
taches, were Corsicans of old stock, men of the bandit days. Their
bearing was proud.

Such pride, such granite unconcern must have proved a formidable barrier to the engineer's commerce. But a barrier that perhaps he welcomed, as many small illnesses are welcomed, for the
passionate pain they provoke. There was no doubt that he was
now in pain. He had pushed his dark glasses on to his forehead,
agonized eyebrows reached up to them like the stretched legs of
frogs, his dark searching eyes glittered, his lips seemed to move in
a motion faster than the flow of words—and all the time that
small wedge of little birds fluttered between his mouth and the
stern eyes of the two disapproving old men. The old men—perhaps owners of a restaurant, perhaps of good wives—were potential
buyers of the robins. One of them said:

'I have offered you six francs the bird.'

He said this without vehemence, as having stated not a price
but some patriarchal law. He said nothing further, only pulled
slowly at a tooth under his moustache. The engineer burst into an
appeal of despair—for ten francs the bird. Ten francs! Ten small
francs for the most savoury, the delicious little bird! Shot even
that morning, fresh from eating the odorous maquis—the exquisite

bird of the red throat!

But obduracy had hardened in the veins of those old men. Many Mediterranean peoples buy, sell, bargain, run after coins bright and round as their sun, run after them without shame and with laughter, even without avarice and only as a reasonable means to an end. These Corsicans are different. Centuries of fighting against imperialists from the mainlands, against Spain and France and always Genoa, have welded them into firm communities, groups of the family and of the village and of the island. Their need was always to be self-provident, independent in their mountains and thence independent in their hearts. That which they own they give freely—but they will fight bitterly if it is snatched by force. Such a pride does not allow them to bargain. They state their view, their fair price. It is the last word.

Infuriating for the sinuous engineer. This one was now driven by his sunsoaked frenzy into a beatification that soon rose far beyond his wares, rose from praising the dead bird to a lyric of the bird alive, the bird he had shot, but of whose life and beauty he was deeply aware. Of course, he exaggerated:

'Fine, the little rouge-gorge! High in the maquis she sits, her breast shines like the red arbutus. Small, yes, but up there in the green it is the only little person that is alive—like a mouse she darts among the low branches.'

As he spoke his eyes rolled, his fingers played with air as lightly as birds' wings—this shooter of birds in the back. But transported now, it was plain that while killing birds he loved them, or knew their live mystery, their freedom. I who while eating flesh condemn any joy in its killing was astounded—it had never occurred to me that you could love these things exactly at the same time as killing, that in fact the processes of loving life and killing it for one's own survival could occur in the same brain at the same time, fully, without the trammelings of pity. To all this the old men just nodded. They too knew.

'There was the sky, blue and wide, the great sky, and up flew the little bird, its red breast shining in the sun, I saw the red, I aimed . . .'

Of course he never saw the red. Nor did he see what I saw— thrushes I had eaten at lunch, little naked birds served whole and still on thick toast. Birds featherless as fledglings, with their beaks and big-lidded eyes shut and saurian, baby pterodactyls. A delicacy, for their flesh was nurtured on the aromatic scrub. Others in the restaurant lifted the birds with their fingers and picked with their teeth at the heads.

'I sprang forward! I picked her up, and she was still warm. See, only this morning, warm and fresh from the herbs of the maquis . . .'

And there he was tacked back again on to his selling course. The flight of fancy was over. But it had been real. He was no poet, he was an engineer and apart from his looks a not uncommon one. Yet, here he was one of a curious breed—the breed of the loving hunter. No regrets, he faced up to the cruelty of life and lived his part of it; and he loved life. An aesthete of the open field, he saw his prey as a thing of beauty. But he saw it according to the scale of his own animality, not with sentiment as a fellow creature. It could only have been love that gave him such joy in killing. He cared much more than on the score of prowess. He cared much more than an ordinary lover of beauty— the debased aesthete who is held to be all heart and sympathy, but who so often becomes the most intolerant of men, a creature refined beyond generous living. But here was the predatory aesthete, a fine mind if a dark one.

However—his words were now of no use—the thoughtful patriarchs rebutted him with their pride. They made no further offer, but simply let him speak himself back into silence. As for him— perhaps he had the whole afternoon to spare and a whole town of buyers to try, or he was defiant on his own terms. In any case, he suddenly turned away, and with a brief word of parting went striding fast round the corner into the afternoon crowd of the Cours Napoléon. I followed. Once round the corner he stopped, undecided. He was still quivering with his extraordinary vehemence, more alive and alight than ever. He paused, one could hear him raging inside: 'Where now, where now with my little robins?' Suddenly he decided; in his awkward but swiftly efficient way he darted away into the crowd, into the mixed moving mass of corduroy and dark blue and Latin black and Senegalese red and all the patched-up khaki that made the fashionable throng of this capital street. He disappeared. But I was to see him frequently throughout the afternoon—before the tumultuous evening ever began.

In such a small town it is difficult to avoid meeting again such an acquaintance—particularly as my own afternoon was spent wandering and looking. Thus I saw him in the market town by the quay, out by the railway station with its earnest small trains winding off up the mountains to the old capital of Corte, in a cool stone restaurant spacious with pots of plants and lean tailless dogs, in a bar whose fixtures were of the Empire's gold and mahogany, in one of the cavernous dark shops sacked with grain and pasta. Each time he was bargaining, brandishing the robins. Not only with the imperturbable Corsican, but with other more vociferous Latins. As the hours passed, so the feathers of the little birds grew fluffed and scragged. But it seemed no one would pay his price; perhaps he deceived himself by applying the higher prices of the mainland to the simpler island economy. It seemed, at all costs, such a small transaction; but the engineer had plainly become obsessed. The transaction had become more important than the profit. Besides, many other small deals could be seen loitering round those streets—there was one tall Senegalese walking slowly from restaurant to restaurant like a priest in his red fez, a single blue-black crayfish weaving its worried feelers from his purple-black hand.

Towards four o'clock the sun grew milky and disappeared, massive clouds came lowering in from the sea. The ochreous town grew pale beneath a giant darkness. An hour later, the storm had still not broken. Still it massed strength, piling up weight upon weight of cloud, darkness upon darkness. It was about then, at five o'clock, that I noticed a crowd taking a direction: everyone seemed to be moving down from the Cours and the big Place towards the harbour, in fact towards another square enclosing yet another statue of Napoléon and at the same time the Hotel de Ville.

It was outside this pillared and balconied seat of government that a large crowd now collected. A newly elected deputy was formally taking over his office. Ajaccio had assembled to acclaim him. Now they waited, strolled, chattered, milled; a feeling of storm, of tense expectation, of suppressed revelry tautened the air —and suddenly all the electric lights were switched on. Wired among the branches of the plane and palm trees covering this little square, the yellow bulbs blazed gaudily, lit up the autumn leaves, cut themselves bright against the slate-dark sky above. Through the tall window of the balcony a glittering glass chandelier shone, telling of rich official pomp, of soft ambassadorial feet within.

All Ajaccio! That hot, seedy crowd gathered to the centre of their sun-soaked town with not much more purpose than just to gather, to stir into life. Throughout those latitudes townspeople gathered for the evening parade, for the strolling and passing and turning about in their thousand twilit squares; but this was more —some came with political feeling, others stirred patriotically, for all there was the expectation of an 'occasion'! So they stood about on the sandy ground under the plane-trees and palms, all eyes on the central yellow building with its chandelier, with its draped swathe of tricolour, with its ionic portico and its old red carpet frayed and holed. Blue-uniformed cadets lined the entrance. A loud-speaker attached to the balcony roared out music from a gramophone—Viennese waltzes, giddying javas, jazz. That loud-speaker seemed to be made all of wire, it grated so. And so also the bell that suddenly chimed five from the clock-tower—a thin wiry bell shrill above the metal music; and the wired feeling of the electric lights among the branches—through the warm air all these makeshift wires galvanised the night. The yellow tower steadily grew paler against the monstrous cloud looming indigo above; soon its stucco seemed to shine against so much darkness; then, from far across the mountains, there flickered sudden violet flashes, like shadows of light growing huge and as swiftly gone— the pagan lightning crossed the mountains with angry leaps, bewildered the electric night.

Such giant violet flickerings made the little square smaller, ex-aggerated the dreadful clarity of those high wide mountain spaces above. The town huddled closer; nursing its shoddiness; boasting its claim with bright-yellow bulbs and loud music. And several little boys were already letting off ground fireworks, so that crim-son and green flares began to colour the crowd, casting fantastic shadows, while small drifts of smoke drifted a light fog here and there.

Napoléon stood moveless in white marble, encircled in his grove of withered palms. Four lions slobbered at his feet, their mouths green with moss over which slow water trickled; it seemed that these lions, snub-faced as pekinese, dropped their saliva as the townsfolk themselves spat, with no ejaculatory effort—it was too hot—only leaning their heads aside and letting the saliva fall. By the railings of this statue a small dark man in khaki plus-fours was tearing up long strips of white paper for makeshift confetti; past him walked two fine dark beauties, black-eyed nubiles of the south, their hair a chemical gold; a group of middle-aged men passed—grey sweaters, brown boots, black hats, silver bristles, striped dusty trousers—and their women with them, shapeless in black; a muscle-chested brown young man in a striped singlet, with a white cap set squarely over his head—the cap had a great white button round as his roving eye; two naval airmen, quiet in their disciplined nonentity, their fear; a large girl with high flat cheek-bones like her thick-boned ankles, as if an olive-skinned Swede; youths slouching quickly, swinging their arms, kicking at odd stones, vigorous and laughing braggishly at each other; a man in khaki breeches and woollen stockings, a motor-racer's leather cap flapping over his ears; Senegalese; Tunisians; Italians; French—and suddenly, thin and knobbly in pale blue came jerking along that engineer! Now his glasses were off. He still held in his hand the bunch of robins.

As he came round the railings and took a course diagonally across the square, his sharp inquisitive face pecked in every direction, his eyes darted everywhere—no one in that whole crowd could have escaped him. Then, as usual, he disappeared into a bar.

This bar lay down towards the sea end of the square, whose lower end was open to the quay. It was a cavern bar, with a wide opening like half a huge egg. When I came in, the engineer had already engaged himself heavily with another man, a short man (they all looked short against his long figure). This man wore a leather motor-coat with a fur collar, American army boots and breeches, a beret. As always the blue képi was lowered down at his face, before which swung the robins. However, this time there was a difference. The engineer now held a glass of pastis in his free hand. Moreover, the shorter man had also taken a glass of pastis, and perhaps more than one. He hardly played his part

in the discussion of the robins correctly, he was unserious, he
smiled, he laughed, he interrupted the engineer to lay an arm on
his shoulder, protesting his delight in seeing his old friend the
engineer, declaiming and pouting his manly love with a puffing
of cheeks and a bracing of biceps. Worse, he praised the robins.

'Oui, mon Dominique, fine birds! Beauties!'

'Eh?'

'Beauties! And good shooting, Dominique, mon cher.'

'Ah. Mm. But you are right. You see them, you know. There's
no more to be said. I'll—'

'Yes, old fellow, good shooting. Dominique knows a rifle. Remember, Dominique, the night at Porto when—'

'For you especially, for you my old friend, I offer them for only
twelve francs the bird. Twelve! No more.'

'—the night you engaged the good macaronis—'

'Listen, Emilio, the birds—'

'Ten macaronis and a beautiful machine gun, phat-ta-ta-tat.
And my Dominique with his old rifle, jumping about in the
dark, firing from here, there and everywhere like twenty men. By
God, you could not blame them.'

'Emilio, I shot them this morning, five of them.'

'Macaronis?'

'Macaronis hell—*red-breasts!*'

'Ah, the beauties.'

'Emilio—ten francs the bird.'

But already Emilio was signing for two more pastis making large
round generous signs with his muscular hands, so that two double
glasses of the milk-white absinth faced them on the zinc. With an
abrupt gesture of impatience the engineer tossed back his first
glass, then took up the new one. For a moment he said nothing,
but looked down darkly at the robins. Emilio went on to talk of
old times in the maquis. Behind them a weak electric light cast
the shadows of its bracket across a wall alive with menacing
shapes, giant brown sunflowers on an oil-green paper. The paper
had been laid over previous embossed decorations, and now
bulged and receded, rose and fell without moving. Two bicycles
stood against a wicker table. Outside, through the dark arch of
the entrance, the Place des Palmiers showed brightness and movement, the crowd was still growing, the flare and smoke of more

fireworks veiled it with a sense of furnaces, of carnival. Music echoed across the warm air like the throbbing steam-music of a fair. Emilio had begun a marching-song.

The engineer suddenly emptied his glass and called for two more. He frowned, and as if making a decision emptied also his new glass of pastis. Then, at the top of his voice, he began trying again to sell the birds to Emilio. He shook the birds savagely. One or two small feathers floated down to the wine-stained floor. But Emilio went on singing, now with closed eyes, feet marching up and down, his forearm bunched to slope an imaginary rifle. So that the engineer Dominique's voice rose also louder, he began to rave. I moved away to the arched door. Emilio, who was neither acting nor insensitive that he was being spoken to, occasionally broke off in the middle of his song to pat the birds and enquire after Dominique's family.

'And your *mother*? How is your *mother*? Lola, how is *Lola*? A big girl? Beautiful?'

'All their lives they have been feeding on a maquis, the herbs. Emilio, eight francs, you rob me.'

Emilio had turned away and was paying much more—sixty francs—for two large pastis. As indeed previously the engineer had done—he who had spent a day trying to sell five birds for about fifty francs. But it was the transaction, not the profit. But now suddenly the arm holding the little birds dropped low, another blue arm reached out to Emilio's neck—and softly, with an oddly open mouth, the engineer began to croon. He sang in a sweet tenor the same song as Emilio, holding tremulously on to the sustained notes. His whole rapacious face took on the look of a thin old woman transported by sentimental thoughts; now wide open, his lips disappeared thinly stretched to show—a shock—that he had no teeth. The black hole of a mouth looked like one black sunglass.

I could hear gusts of their talk—for every so often they stopped singing and, embracing, exchanged greetings and reminiscence. The glasses of pastis, strong drink of wormwood that first tastes weak, came and went. They grew more and more friendly. Sometimes one said:

'Eh, Dominique!'

While the other, leaning back the better to survey his old

friend, would intone his reply with a frown of loving bravado:

'Emilio!'

Outside, the tension had reached some sort of climax—the appearance of the deputy seemed to be due. The crowd had grown thick round the portico of the hotel, I could see the brass instruments of a band flashing dully about the bottom steps. From this centre the square beneath those trees was forested with groups of people, black against the lights, against the whitish firework smoke. Not a crowd dense as in a great city, but a large crowd dispersed, populating the whole square. The plane branches and their dried November leaves made a ceiling of the electric light, such foliage looked papery, like illuminated theatrical trees. Such a ceiling a few feet above the people's heads existed throughout all the twenty-four hours of all southern towns—in daytime the leaves enclosed with shade the pavement, while all light and energy lay high in the sunlit air above; at night at the same level the shade became reversed, the dark inactive night stretched its black vacuum above, while beneath the same low ceiling all was light and movement.

'Chestnut cakes at Piana—remember? Fresh from the wood!'

'The Rizzanese—a real river that, fine cold water!'

> 'Ah! le petit vin blanc—
> Qu'on boit sous les tonnelles.'

Now they were singing together the generous little waltz-tune. Their movement as they swayed, as the engineer beat time with his bunch of birds, seemed, with the sound of their singing, to fill the dark little bar. Outside night had not yet fallen. There was still in the air, besides the occasion and the music and the fireworks, that excitement, that air of prelude that charges the twilight air with promises of night. Against now a sky the colour of dark iron, the façades of the buildings shone incandescently white, pearl-coloured, pale as bone. Only the decorated Hôtel de Ville broke the regularity of these square façades with their black regular windows; the Hôtel de Ville with its clock-tower, its coat-of-arms, its ionic pillars, its balcony, its brave draping of the blue, white and red flag of France.

'Emilio, old friend, listen! A mark of esteem in honour of our meeting, in celebration of the Deputy. His Honour. Emilio—a

gift—I *give* you the birds!'
  'Uh?'
  'The birds, my little robins! I give them to you.'
  'What?'
  'For nothing!'
  'Eh?'
  'There, take them.'
  'But . . . well, many thanks. Many, many thanks.'
  'Ah!'
  'But—'
  'Yes?'
  'But Dominique, my Dominique—'
  'Ah! le petit vin blanc.'
  'But Dominique, I cannot take them. I must pay. Here, fifty francs.'
  'No!'
  'Forty francs.'
  'You insult me!'
  'Take twenty.'
  'If you insist.'
  'There!'
  'Now. Permit me to offer you a pastis.'
  A murmur came from the crowd, and this rose to a shout. Behind me the singing stopped. Those two had heard the shout. Now with cries of 'the Deputy!' they were running past me and out through the door. Through the crowd they dodged, the long engineer first, Emilio on shorter legs zigzagging behind. They ran like children, like enthused students—not worrying whom they bumped, laughing and letting arms and jacket flap wildly. The engineer's arms were free, he no longer held his robins.
  Over by the steps now everyone and everything had collected. A passage had been cleared by cadets and police. Down this the old red carpet, dusty and holed, stretched its royal channel. As it finished, so there began the band, an elderly and jovial group of players in assorted clothes—from plus-fours to breeches of corduroy—but each wearing a dark jacket and an old peaked cap. They looked like railwaymen; but each held proudly his brass or silver instrument, and one man was already bent backwards against the weight of his big brass drum. Several small boys ran

about in the aisle carrying white boards on sticks. On the boards were written 'Vive la République!' and 'Criez le 20 Octobre!'. And on all sides the crowd, old and young, men and women, pressed forward, singing, jostling, shouting, and all waving long strips of white paper.

A brief hush. Movements occurred at the back of the hall inside. The loudspeaker music abruptly stopped. The band raised their instruments to their lips. And on the steps there emerged the deputy and a little procession of officials.

At the same moment the loudspeaker above the balcony burst into music louder, faster, wilder than any before. But it was not the Marseillaise, nor a Corsican anthem, nor any martial song at all. There came the hot thunderous cacophony of negroes— 'Washboard Blues!'. Simultaneously the band began to play—but only the loud thumping of the big drum could be heard above the loudspeaker. The procession began to move down the steps and away. Instantly—for the crowd stood only three feet off on either side—they were mobbed. The air flew with white paper strips. A hundred arms reached forward to touch the deputy. Shouts, cheers, wild whistling. From all sides a battery of fireworks burst—green, yellow, Mephistophelian red. Through all this, the procession struggled away as it could, fighting through the smoke and colour and laughter, then turned sharply right into the Rue Fesch. The famous old street, narrow and winding, was filled to the walls of its tall houses with a jostling mass. All along its serpentine way the people crammed. Away in front, growing dimmer, the beat of the big drum echoed. After it, flexing like a dragon, wound the procession of all Ajaccio. Banners swayed, arms tossed hats high, the dragon swarmed waddling on a thousand unseen legs.

Then I saw for the last time that tall blue képi—higher than the rest of the crowd but caught in it, laughing and fighting and struggling as he was borne along, as now he receded from me, dragged away, drowned it seemed in the moving swelling devouring sea, the sea of hats, caps, fezzes, hands, arms, faces . . .

I walked back to the bar. There on the floor half beneath the wicker table lay the little robins, ruffled, deflated, their skinny eyelids closed tight, their short beaks shut, and all around like bright puffs of dust the small feathers.

Eventide

Six o'clock. A cold summer's evening.

The bar was empty. Polished linoleum slid over the floor and the clock was stopped—not a tick to disturb the dustless quiet of dark shamrock curtains, dark-varnished wood, windows paned in neat squares of frosted glass: nothing glittered; all only shone dully in the grey evening light, and such gloom could not even be called subaqueous, it was so dry and dead. Yet this was the saloon bar of a public house; and now at six o'clock sat waiting, its clock stopped, for time to pass.

After a long while the door pressed open. The door never swung, there was a compressed air device screwed to the top, and a rubber wheel ensured further quiet. A man came in. First he was a shadow against the street light, then a man in a creased grey suit walking to the bar—as the door, his accomplice, bowed to a rubbery close behind him.

From behind the bar half a woman shot up, a cardiganed torso on a sudden spring-lift, glasses masking her eyes, cheek-bones gleaming white, a net dowsing dull brown hair. She stood facing the man, thin-lipped. Neither spoke.

The man stood chest-on to the bar, feet placed astride, planted like a passenger on a ship. He now sighed, as if a journey had been completed. He took a big sheet of a handkerchief from his pocket, buried his face in it, and blew. With no more than a quick glance at what he had blown, he braced his shoulders again and sucked in air through his teeth. Glancing sharply to left and right at the emptiness, making sure they were alone, again he faced the woman, who had been waiting, rigid and woolly, all this time.

Finally the man said: 'Good evening'.

He cooed the 'good' high and the 'evening' low, so that it made a little song—but not so much a song of greeting as a lullaby of condolence.

The woman made no spoken reply. But her head inclined in the shade of a small bob, recognizing the greeting as an item ticked off on a list.

The man then took a pipe from his pocket, looked at it, shook it, and set it into his teeth so that it stuck out upside down like an odd piece of brown plumbing.

It must have given his molars a clenched, manly feel—he sucked in air again with a big-chested hiss: and now he said, as if it were all one long slow word:

'Nice-glasser-best-Mrs-S.'

He spoke as if he had turned the condolence in upon himself: he ordered this beer not as if he desired it but as if he deserved it, and that it was not all he deserved, but he would be quite satisfied to accept it, he was not the man to ask for too much, his demands were reasonable and modest. Enough was quite enough for him. For the present. And nobody should deny it.

He was balding a little, thin sandy hair looked stranded over red ears, and his pale office-whipped face had a pleasing mildness. He received his drink, paid for it, fingering out the exact money, and remained standing, not touching the glass, satisfied simply by its presence.

Then again silence.

As he contemplated the glass, the woman returned to her evening paper. The clock stared paralysed. Only the little pipe, upside down cast a note of brown caprice into a scene otherwise still as death.

There would be hours of daylight yet. Double summer time had stolen the sundown hour. Day's work ended, evening begun had lost its proper definition of approaching darkness: it was a neutral time.

The saloon bar had been furnished in the 'thirties in an attempt to be homely and be cheerful. A note once modern had impaled itself on the air once and forever, delineating time the more strongly for its recent passing—sad and near as the death of a promising child, and, in terms of the world and the passing years, as expendable.

The hopes, the abundant feeling that must have gone to make such a place! A horizontal oval mirror hung on thin brass chains over the fireplace. The fireplace itself had square mauve tiles that shone but did not reflect, and they were surrounded again by dark stained wood. A gas-pipe, bright-polished, fled like a killer-snake from the ladylike fender. The fire itself bared its boney sockets like a death-trap.

The dark wood that everywhere predominated had a cheap brittle texture, a sense of varnished creosote. Even the dart-board was nicely enclosed in a dark wood cabinet. Someone had had the ideas 'sunny' and 'cheerful'—there was a dado of whipped-up copper-brown plaster waves and above this a wallpaper of embossed gamboge shells: the effect was of the awful yellow glow that precedes a great tropic storm, the colour of the end of the world.

Spattered about were cheerful trifles: paintings of Cornish fisher-villages, a gold basket sprouting paper flowers, cardboard beermats. Advertisement cards mounted on their own props snapped and yelped.

But no room could be so uniformly dreadful as this: there was indeed one note of relief that might have cheered the trapped customer. On one window appeared in bright red letters the lightly mad, enchanting message: TUOTƧ.

Suddenly the woman behind the bar closed her paper with a rustle like a thunderclap.

'You don't know my biggest boy,' she said. 'He's grown a beard.'

The man looked anxious. 'There now,' he said, and clutched the pockets at the side of his coat. And then the woman began to fish urgently in her bag. Her breathing got short. The man looked more than ever anxious. He peered over. Would she find it, what was it, would it be lost forever?

But she suddenly snapped out a bruised brown wallet. 'Here we are,' she said and bent her glasses down fingering at photographs inside. She drew out two of these. One she put on the bar for the man to see. It showed a young cleanshaven sailor smiling against a brick barrack building.

'That's how he is really,' said the woman and then showed him the other photograph, of a similar young sailor, but with a beard.

'And that's how he really is,' said the woman.

The man nodded. They both gazed at the photographs, at little grey different worlds somewhere far away where the sun had once shone.

'He's a sailor,' the woman explained.

'Ah,' the man said.

And the silence like a hungry black spore came gliding up from nowhere and gathered itself hammering huge. It had waited like dust in this room where there was no speck of real dust, and now it rained down dry dew all over them. The man struggled to say something—but the silence was falling too heavy.

Then at the last moment his eye caught a picture in the paper she had put down. His short fat forefinger came from his pocket and like a squat sausage held in his hand pointed all by itself at the representation of a kingfisher.

'We had one of them come in the garden once,' he said. 'Little blue bird.'

He raised his eyebrows and smiled straight at the woman. Her glasses stared back reflecting nothing. The silence began to shroud over again.

'Went away after a couple of days,' the man sighed. 'Never saw it no more.'

And down clapped the silence. The man raised his glass and slid some of the beer down inside him. It made no sound whatever. The woman picked up the photographs and tucked them away. A thin sunbeam slid in over a patch of linoleum, shivered, turned grey, and disappeared.

But twenty minutes later the door opened and one, two, three, four quite separate people came in. A train might have arrived, disgorging sudden passengers. Yet there was no train near, nor any particular bus.

However, men with briefcases and umbrellas and hats and a woman with a string bag bulging tins all came in and scattered themselves everywhere, there was shuffling of shoes and a cracking of papers, a tinkling of glass and a fizzing of soda-water; and the little light of cigarettes lit; and talk.

They exchanged civilities. They said about the weather. One of the men winked and murmured, 'Mind how you go' to the woman with the string bag raising gin to her lips.

There was nothing said that had not been said a hundred million times before. Yet how precious, how preposterous a load of lovely human litter, like a confetti of coloured bus tickets! How warmly and lightly these simple communications hit upon the air!

Even the death of the furniture died away.

The man in the grey suit coughed, eased his shoulders as if throwing off a chill, blew out a deep breath of relief and suddenly winked and leaned across to the woman behind the bar.

'And how is that boy of yours these days,' he said, 'your sailor-boy with the beard?'

Where Liberty Lies

Nowadays we bump into far fewer of our friends in the street, we no longer walk so much about the street, we spend our time jammed into little cars. Not so often now the joy of a chance meeting, the smile and the raised hat, the dark pleasure of cutting our enemies. In some parts of America you will quickly be arrested for not being jammed in a car: walking is suspected as loitering, and that will be our own future if we do not look out, and get out and walk.

It must have been when I started walking again that I first met Rodney. Rodney—he never seemed to have a surname, he was a recognised 'case', a queer fellow addressed by all sorts of knowing people quite affectionately by his first name, with a kindly neigh, as if it were a nickname—Rodney walked a lot. Hardly a day seemed to pass when you would not see him lumbering up the Charing Cross Road, strolling in Piccadilly, limping up Harley Street, or just echoing along one of the many underground passages into which pedestrians have to go to avoid bumping into people jammed into little cars.

I noticed him first in the public library, where for a time my work sent me. I was there in search of that dear old double-act, wolfram and tungsten; he in search of free heat. He had a birdy-looking face, much nose and little mouth, and with eyes quick to glance everywhere through the owl-rings of his Health spectacles —a thrush of a man in a neat brown suit, with pale grey hair and a trim scrub of short grey beard. He had the waist of a youth of twenty, a cavity instead of a stomach. He was all knuckles and shine. His movements were agile and quick, and he turned his feet far out as he pounced along. He was essentially neat—there was nothing of the usual library eccentric about Rodney, no patches, no string, no poring through magnifying glasses, no newspaper lunch beside him, no muttering. He was neat and precise, he might have been the head librarian himself. Certainly he acted like one. One day when I arrived very early, the first in the library, with my books already stretched out on the polished oak table, I was surprised to find this bird-faced figure standing above me and telling me I was in his place.

'But there were no books here? How is it your place?'

'Because I was sitting there. Be so good as to . . .' and the *Handyman's Encyclopaedia* was placed authoritatively beside my own books, ready to take their place.

'You left nothing here to mark your seat. This is a *public* library.'

'Peopled, I hope,' he said, 'with the public-spirited. I had simply got up to change my book.'

'Yet . . .' I began, looking round at so much empty space.

'Yet!' he said scornfully at this useful little word. 'Some would not have bothered to return the book to the shelves. Some people would have left a book they no longer wanted, simply to mark their place. I, however, took the trouble to return the book. In case others might need it.'

It was a lie, because I had been there on the stroke of nine.

'Still,' I said, 'there was nothing to show . . .'

'Do you expect me to litter the place with hats and coats?'

'Well, no,' I said.

'Well no!' he said triumphantly.

'You could sit somewhere else . . .' I began.

'This is my place,' he said firmly.

I realised I was in the presence of obsession: but not, until later, also that of the best radiator in the room. I gave in and moved along.

It must have been after this that I kept bumping into Rodney all over the town. A warm Spring had come overnight, and Rodney had left the library. Consciously I would have forgotten about him, as he would have forgotten about me. But most of us know the curious exhilaration that comes with the coincidence of noting one particular stranger time and again in all the millions milling in a large town—how strange, how marvellous! Not at all marvellous. We have simply picked on a chronic walker. So with Rodney. And because I kept on recognising him I began to think I knew him—a friend whom I could not immediately place? —and nodded when we met. At first I received in return a look of dark suspicion. But soon the same illusion must have affected him, for he too began to nod back. We soon became nodding aquaintances. And one day, when winter came, there was my bird-man half-asleep again over the *Handyman's Encyclopaedia* in his warm corner, and we exchanged our first friendly words.

Me: Coming out for a smoke? There's a pub round the corner.

Rodney: There's a hot pipe in the basement. It's free.

And to the basement, by a great python of a pipe, on a stone floor and among dark-green institutional walls leading to the boiler-room, we smoked—myself tobacco, he a half-stub of colts-foot. It was a symbolic introduction. Not only to the economy of Rodney's ways, but also to his particular manner of integrity: although he lived by preying on institutions, he would never cadge from an aquaintance as much as a single cigarette which he could not, or would not like to, return.

Rodney's eccentricity was centred on almost farcical methods of economy—'almost' because all his methods finally worked, and thus could never altogether be laughed off as a joke. He took, for instance, his electricity straight off the main, with recourse to neither meter nor bill. His one basement room, which he rented for near to nothing under some out-of-date agreement, was littered with an alibi of empty oil lamps and heaters; but through the area and into the cellar, and there lay the main—and his simple lead arrangement. He learned it, he told me, from air-raid days when many Londoners, finding themselves huddled down in unheated coal-cellars, had adopted and proved this method. He had neither a bathroom nor a hot water tap: the latter was available in any decent museum, with soap; and as for a bath, in the first place he hated to lose his natural oils, and secondly he could always get a free one from the Council by simulating scabies, in which he was helped by the symptoms of an easily boosted urticaria. And so on. He had even once borrowed an electric blanket on which to cook a perfect thirty-six hour *boeuf bourgogne*, but had finally laughed himself out of this— for he was only economising with the company's fuel. Even so it had saved him the bother of finding an asbestos sheet for his

little electric ring: and his sense of thrift ran so deep that he really
enjoyed the saving for its own sake.

He was, of course, a bachelor. 'The only free man living almost
free'—he used to boast in his quiet way. 'And if anyone else
comes with that two-can-live-cheaper-than-one lark, I'll break a
blood vessel if I can borrow one. Two people,' he said, 'never
want the same thing at the same time—one wants a cup of Oxo
so out of companionship the other has a cup too. Now is that one
or two cups of Oxo? That other one might not have thought of
Oxo not for hours, days even. That's how it goes. You may halve
your rent, but you double your wear and tear and all your con-
sumptions go up, like with the Oxo.'

'Well, how's your sex-life?' O'Toole or the Sikh or Billy Doux
might ask. These three worked on a building site and used to
come, muddy and battered with rude health, into the café where
Rodney and I sometimes shared a cup of coffee, one cup.

Rodney said quickly, 'I lead a very full sex-life'.

'Hee-hee-hee,' tittered the Sikh in a tiny treble, showing very
small white teeth in a big bearded brown face, turbanned and
bunned, that looked as if it would tear your throat right out in
one bite.

Rodney went on equably: 'When I was a young warden-about-
town in the war, and the flower of Britain's youth away square-
bashing, I had more greens than you've had hot dinners. Until
the Yanks came. But no fooling, by the time the Yanks
came to take over, I'd had all I wanted to show me there's more
in the game than just—well, it showed me you've got to go for
class. What am I doing, I said to myself, with this bit of Bayswater
bint when the town's crammed with rare crumpet suitable for Top
People? But class, just even to be with class, costs money. And I
wasn't going to work myself to the bone not for a mad night with
a mink. No, I looked around and I said, 'What are these Top
People doing all the time with this Top Crumpet of theirs? Taking
it around with them, I see. *Talking* to it. Spending time with it.
Letting it talk to *them*, too. Restaurants, walks, drives, dances—
and keeping their eye on other minks while they're doing it. Now
these Top People are not wasting their time on all this just for
five minutes later on with the lady in her birthday suit. For when
you've stripped 'em what have you got? Just another birthday

suit and what you've done is stripped theirselves off of them, because it's theirselves all dressed up that's the real mink. So don't tell me those cut-throats with their sales-charts and their costing complexes spend all these hours for five minutes with a birthday suit, it's against nature. No, they *like* it.'

'Go on,' says O'Toole, 'you're working me to death.'

Billy Doux's dark Caribbean lids closed over his yellow eyeballs. 'Fine feathers, man.' Billy got his name for giving up a soft job at the top of the down tube escalator standing there not having to clip tickets. It was too indolent a work even for a full-grown West Indian man, it drove him to laying bricks.

'Fine feathers is right, Billy,' Rodney said. 'So what do I do?' Rodney said. 'I'll have a piece of this, I say, without paying a sou. Right now I'm enjoying the company of three of the finest birds in this town. All you have to do is station yourself outside the back entrance of a modelling house, and out they come. Or in Bond Street around noon of a Spring morning, when the class goes window shopping. I just watch 'em: which is about all the Top People do anyway. I don't undress them with my eyes, I'm not that daft. No, I want the best and I get it. Concentration's the secret. When I watch them I *watch*. Do I worry when they don't smile at me? I'm above vanity, thank you. Do I worry that I don't hear what they have to say? You know the answer to that one. No, boy, I'm sitting pretty. *And* I don't have to stay up all night. I can get a bit of shut-eye.'

O'Toole shook his head in wonder. 'Don't you feel a bit lonely when you get home nights?' he said.

'I've got me pin-ups,' Rodney said.

'But they don't talk, they don't . . .'

'Talk!' Rodney shouted. 'D'you think I want them pin-ups bawling my head off all bloody night?'

'Hee-hee-hee,' tittered the Sikh. And so it went on, the amiable misunderstanding of worker and workless, the three workers from the scaffolding opposite—slaves, Rodney called them—and the Soul of Free Enterprise. Or Sole, as they began to call him, for one of Rodney's few almost insoluble problems was shoe-leather—of which he used a lot. He partially solved this with cut-outs from old rubber tyres, but a serviceable adhesive had to be borrowed—and the boys on the building lot got him this. A problem soluble only with rubber solution, though it sometimes cost him a humiliating cup of coffee.

The building trade is good for all manner of raw material. Rodney had learned his scrounging in the war. He appreciated the difference between scrounging and stealing: the one carried an affirmative virtue, the other was plain idiotic for the penalties it invited. But in his warden's war, he had been thrown in with many an old ex-serviceman who spent the dull lull hours in making something of nothing—a cigarette lighter from a cartridge case, a balaclava from a discarded stocking, a portrait of Hitler, entirely from old bits of string. This period, as with his sex-life, had done much to form him—he could not bear to pass over a single broken bit of anything without pocketing it for a future sunny day. To top this—and it is of course a cardinal point— Rodney had a private income of four pounds a week. This put the crowning seal on his liberty.

So he went his ways, viewing television in shop windows—so much better without the sound. The wireless news he heard from an electric-parts shop window—he could have run a wireless on free current, but there were repairs to consider. Every so often he would have a real blow-out at a Cookery School. Otherwise food was indeed an expense. But he begged bones and beefskirt for the doggie, a whole big saucepanful for a penny, and kept himself well in soup. 'Lights for the cat' he cooked with basil and thyme in the Greek manner.

Rodney off for his morning wash in the Victoria and Albert Museum! A brisk walk through the empty park, head pecking from side to side at every flower and tree—he knew each one personally as if these were his own private acres—and down into the lavatory, where piping hot water and big brass taps awaited him. Decent big basins and space here—none of your plastic box bathrooms. A good rub on the towelmaster, and he was up for a brief glance at an exhibit or two. Knowledge he loved: it had the merits of both acquisition and luxury.

Rodney off to visit a few new friends! A visit to a house-agent and the addresses of a couple of good furnished flats . . . a ring on the bell at about tea-time, and there was a whole new private world of furniture and Life to inspect, and a fine understanding housewife to hand him a cup of tea (Oh no, I really *can't*! Well, just a little then, sugar, yes please four lumps') and possibly toast. A polite housewife too, for he was a prospective buyer; and in any case was she not proud to be showing off her old furniture to a new face? And to have a new ear for the salient points of her family history? Though Rodney kept his earflaps well down, he was past-master at nodding and putting a weird brightness into his old eye.

Rodney planning a holiday abroad! Into the travel agents for a mass of free pamphlets, a long discussion of ways and means with often the most exotic ladies from Italy, Greece, Ireland. Then back home to bask in a sunshine more vivid than the reality of those places. Finally, out to the telephone and a call to the airline office to arrange a ticket, again a long discussion as to dates and times and the final and true exhilaration of making the provisional booking. Naturally it was never confirmed. Why should Rodney have to go all that way, suffer sunburn, dysentery, boredom and so on?

Rodney on his *real* annual holiday! The venue, a comfortable hospital in the country or by the sea. With a terrace large enough to hold a good wheeled day-bed, and, God willing, a free show of a kind, echoes from the summer bandstand, a few thousand tons of good shipping on the horizon, a harvest of tractors on up-hill fields, an elmful of rooks. Predicting the weather as best he could, Rodney would first go into training—eat nothing for a week but perhaps fruit or a boiled onion. 'Every man his own hydro,' he would say, 'a necessity for Top People and in my case a few guineas cheaper without the fatigue of a lot of other Top People'. Simultaneously he would take extra long walks to swell up his feet. He never minded the walking which an indisposition to paid transport cost him—he thought of it as what it was, sensible and non-violent exercise for a man of his years: again an attitude of mind, making of a necessary imposition a voluntary benefit. When his feet were swollen enough, he would hitchhike to his chosen Kentish or Sussex resort, walk to the hospital, throw a fit, and be entered. The weakness of a week's starvation, the feet and a number of other small tricks ensured him a good convalescence. He would return to London well-rested and brown as a fiddle.

So he went his way, visiting the cinema by the side push-bar entrance as others came out, writing off for free samples, amassing an impressive private culture from galleries and museums made free to the public. A biting aroma of burned coltsfoot hung where he had passed, as though a herby ghost were abroad, and he made a close study of the habits of cats—learning from them such important trivia as the flow of a draught and the warmest corner, the amount of heat flooding from a heavy watt electric bulb, the real warmth of newspaper. Thus his easy chair was raised high off the ground with a high footstool, the reading lamp placed directly behind to warm the back of his neck, the whole thing padded out with a massing of old news. It was interesting that he learned of the warmth of newspaper from cats rather than the down-and-out human tramp—his eyes were raised always upwards.

His ordinary practical knowledge was immense—he would come back from a hitch in the country packed with edible fungi, he knew rivers close to London crawling with crayfish, he brought home the right snails and he grew his own penicillin and his own mushrooms in the coal cellar: on a warm September day he would stand in the Essex mud and gorge himself on clams, and there was even a time when he strewed the basement area with cheese-rind, netted it against cats, fattened and then trapped an army of mice, and stewed them sweetly in the Chinese manner. But this, and the liming of sparrows for a 'Corsican toast', passed. He was always on to something new, always on the go, go go.

And this go, go, go, at first deceptive, did not finally pass unchallenged. One day, when he had returned from a night at a Home Counties rehabilitation centre with a fine new suit, and was sharing my cup of coffee, O'Toole on the other side of the caff began sniffing the air loudly and looking across at us—Rodney in fact, was higher in scent than the combined smell of kippers and fat fry.

'Hello,' O'Toole said. 'And who's the gallant British Hommy? Pooh.'

I knew what Rodney was at. But of course he had to tell O'Toole in detail. Usually we accepted from Rodney what would sound like intolerable boasting from another man. His was the innocence of the obsessed. He was like a naughty old child. But occasionally it did get irritating—as one becomes slightly envious of, and thus irritated with, a too precocious child.

'I've been along to a nice warm perfume department not a hundred miles from Oxford Street,' he said, 'getting well squirted by the nice girls there—it's mostly *Chanel 5* and *Je Reviens*, they put it on my wrists and palms, but I said it wasn't quite me— and now I'm going to the nice warm writing room of an hotel not a hundred miles from Park Lane to get some correspondence done. I run out of note-paper. A good stink puts them off the scent.'

And, of course, looking so ordinary and orderly and smelling like a night in old-world Bucharest, he would stroll in over the carpets, never faltering, and manage this.

'My God, Rodney,' O'Toole shouted, 'you're the damned hardest worker I've ever met. You ought to take a real job like us and rest up a bit.'

'Hee-hee-hee,' the Sikh tittered, shaking like a hairy jelly.

'Ha ha,' Rodney said.

'Billy Doux here,' said O'Toole emphatically, pointing to the half-closed eyelids beside him, 'has been waiting all afternoon for his bricks to arrive. And half the morning he's been leaning on a spade, a real friend of his. Now he's only waiting for the hooter to blow to collect his pay.'

'Man, it's Friday,' Billy's warm blue lips managed to drawl.

'You're a great one for a joke, Paddy,' Rodney said, 'you bloody slave.'

'Remember the war, Rodney?'

'What d'you mean?'

'Remember all the responsibilities you didn't have? Remember life being lifted right off your shoulders?'

'Not off mine, it wasn't. Though I never heard it called a shoulder before.'

'Life for us is like one lovely long war without the awful need to run. All we do is clock on, a day's healthful exercise or healthy rest, and clock off. The clock tells us what. No looking at watches all day. No questions asked.'

Rodney rose: 'Healthful exercise is what I always say about my walks—'

'Yes, but what about up there?' Billy said tapping the long mindless horizontal lines on his brown brow.

'Up there,' said Rodney, tapping his own thoughtful vertical lines. 'I don't listen for no clocks, I think out what *I* want to do.'

'All day long, all day long,' O'Toole said, 'while Billy here passes the day with a beautiful big blank mind brown as the great urnfuls of tea he needs to keep the sandman at bay . . . why, I read once where a rich society hostess does more work a day fixing things up and dressing and undressing than a cartload of horses, and I laughed—but you're teaching me, boy, you're teaching me.'

The steam rose from the kitchen behind, the green walls dripped beads of it down over red Coca-Cola placards, the great muddy boots came and went browning an old *Daily Mirror* lying black and white on the boards. Rodney was breathing hard, he was rolling his eyes and his knuckles were white as eight more little eyeballs.

'After it's snowed,' he suddenly shouted, 'when it thaws, I go out after dog business.'

'Er?' O'Toole said.

'You don't get your society hostess doing that do you?' Rodney shouted.

'Not on a Wednesday,' O'Toole said slowly, playing for time.

'Nor on her Tuesday,' Rodney roared. 'When it's all piled up with snow, the doggies can't get to their walls and kerbs where they like to drop a bit, they can't find their kerbs and walls, let along manage, so they do it easy on any old bit of snow. Does *that* sink in, O'Toole? I'll say it sinks, it's gone and nobody ever sees it. Not until the thaw comes and then it's all there for the early bird—and that's when I'm out with my shovel and bucket and back in to make compost out the back and there's a fine manure for my herbs and another year's cigarettes.'

'I always said you smoked shit,' O'Toole shouted back.

Rodney hammered his brow: 'Thought!' he yelled, 'free thought! While you slave away God knows how high up there to get the dough to get the tobacco to kill you long before you're in a decent twilight home.'

'Manual *and* mental work, work, double-work,' O'Toole shouted. 'You're worker *and* boss you great stinking ape!'

'I'm free!' yelled Rodney.

'You're double-whipped,' yelled O'Toole.

'I *think,*' rising and punching himself on the forehead, 'I live in my head!'

'That overcrowded slum,' O'Toole shouted.

Rodney lowered his voice and enunciated slowly: 'It-shows-I'm-not-an-animal.'

O'Toole was silent. He stood opposite Rodney and looked him up and down. At last he spoke:

'And what's so fine about that?'

Just then the hooter went—a great throaty organ-pipe made of dustbin-lid moo-ing in all earholes for miles around and clutching at people's stomachs like an air-raid. The Sikh blew out a little sigh:

'Tee-hee-hee,' he said, and got up to go.

And they all got up and went.

'Sheep,' Rodney muttered; then quickly looked up at the clock: 'Heavens, I better get along,' he said, rising quickly.

He must only then have seen what he was doing. It was his moment of truth. Not O'Toole telling him—that he would have fought. Now it was himself telling him himself, suddenly seeing himself hurrying to work, and once again he struggled for breath, and this time he did not get it, he went red and white and then blue and staggered and before my very eyes, as if it were a judgement upon him, he really threw the fit he had so often simulated on the steps of marine or rural hospitals.

It was a long five minutes before the ambulance came. But we had him round. At least he was able to open his eyes and give his last hopeful orders to the driver:

'Bexhill,' he breathed. 'Bexhill . . .'

But it was to the deep warm basement of Charing Cross Hospital he went, and he stayed there, slightly paralysed, for two months. Yet this happened to coincide exactly with the two months of London's great freeze-up.

Rodney never saw an icicle or a burst pipe: he was out again in full blossom with the Spring, though not so greyly placid, a little yellowish, a little purple, like a late flowering crocus.

The Day The Lift . . .

A sudden sense of urgency in the empty office vestibule, a clip-clop of feet hurrying, and round the dusty green-painted corner came trotting a tubby young middle-aged man. Up and down went the feet, not at a run but more as a deference to punctuality—he could have walked as fast to the lift gates in the time.

Who knew—somebody floors above might in the next second press the bell, summoning the lift on its slow ascent upwards: and then a long wait, as whoever it was had a last-minute chat, keeping the lift door open and neutralised. There might even be some tedious porter or clerk ready to load in cartons. Cartons! His legs pranced up higher—but when he got to the black grill of gates the lift was not there at all.

A.B. Bowlsend black-lettered on his brown briefcase, Arnold Brinsley Bowlsend in his mind, pressed the brass bell and listened up the shaft. Not a sound. He quietly cursed and flicked out his wristwatch, a fine commuter's platform flick. But no—his train was not late. Nicely on time. Only that maniac above with the cartons could upset things. Though there was nothing much to upset—his appointment up-shaft was of only routine importance: nothing could be upset but conceptions of order and punctuality, which A.B. Bowlsend of 12 Kelmscott Rise, Thotham, Middx valued and clung to. Bowlsend's life was nicely ordered. He had his wife, two big Bowlsend daughters, his house, car and garden. He had a milieu, he had a street round the corner with a red postal box, another street with a bus-stop, and another close by with older trees to make a pleasant walk. Settled. Under-an-hour to his office. It was a settled state which he was indeed pleased to conserve, and this could first be done by attending to matters which were within practical reach like punctuality—the Lord alone could take care of all those financial and military dangers looming in a limbo of newsprint, they were ever-present but also ever-distant; he himself, a voter, democratically a force in the big world ha ha, could do little about waxing bombs, waning savings. He could, though, be certain about mending a garden fence, warning his sixteen-year-old Marlene on the putative perils of promiscuous youth; and getting up the lift-shaft. He attended to those things he could, he cultivated his garden. Others, the jet lot in their bullet-shaped cars, puffing away at pot and swigging champagne, could scoff at the suburban life: but a greater man than they, Voltaire himself, had commended the garden.* Bowlsend, not yet forty, fit as a fiddle and fairly provident, was happy to stay by this advice.

Good that the lift bell was brass, and had plainly been polished that very day: bright, in fact, as a button. The only light of efficiency in this grimy vestibule with its greyed classic cornices, its green institutional paint, its furnitureless invitation to dust and dirt. The bell would have been cleaned by a janitor, and thus the lift itself would be supervised—had it been out of order, a notice must have said so. Bowlsend knew it to be an old-fashioned kind of lift, and somehow the more trustworthy for this: you were not shut up blind with rubbery air noises in this solid, stately, iron-grilled affair.

He leaned forward and pressed the button again. In doing so, his face leaned closer to the open-grill gates, and the great, oily, black ground-machinery of the lift came intimately into view. Furred with dust like thick soot, darkly greased, all set down in a pit like something lying beneath a railway platform. Heavy stuff, he was glad to see. Reliable. But it was terribly dirty, there must be years of this dust blackened by oil and grease—and somehow bits of paper and cigarette cartons had been thrown there. Imagine flipping a cigarette pack through the gates! Some litter-lout's annoyance at being kept waiting, Bowlsend supposed. But even then a janitor should have cleaned it up? Perhaps it was even the janitor's own mess? So he was not such an efficient man after all? Had his lapses?

However, there was not much wrong with an odd bit of paper. Though Bowlsend was not so sure about plastics. A plastic carton of some kind was a lasting matter. Tough, durable—a crumpled sliver could thoroughly gum up the works? Say, fly in between the steel hawsers and the wheel flange, throttle it? His mind went back to a southern beach, to the picturesque Italian peasant

*See the conclusion to *Candide*—Voltaire (1758).

women carrying their picturesque washing down to the picturesque fresh spring water under the cliff, and the whole mile-long
curve of beach beyond them bobbing with an infrangible bright
yellow band of picturesque detergent bottles. Bottles one, two
years old—even the great salt sea, which eats iron, could not
destroy them.

Still, he thought, where the thing actually worked was clean
and bright—the wheel-flange glinted its rubbed silver, the
hawsers were rustless and greased, though surely a little too
thin, or frail, to take such a weight? Bowlsend muttered the
reassuring word 'tensile', and averted his eyes.

'Lover-boy,' his wife Samantha had said last night, 'looks real,
real cool,' as they changed for dinner.

Which, he had suddenly thought, was a real square echo of a
string-of-pearls lady complimenting her husband's cool dinner
jacket. But Samantha meant cool in an up-to-the-minute sense,
for the Bowlsends religiously changed for dinner each night not
into evening clothes but into fashionable casual garments of
many colours. Like a thousand others, he put off his office suit
and she her housewifely shopping frock to emerge like butterflies
in the latest loungerie as pictured in coloured magazines.
Emerged, they sat about with glasses of some up-to-the-minute
concoction—a mint shandy, vermouth punch—and admired each
other, and felt secure in this the unconventional which had
become a convention.

'Square,' he had suddenly said last night, 'we've come full
circle, we're square,' thinking of dinner jackets and evening
gowns.

He had tried to explain, but neither his wife nor two galumph-
ing daughters—also arrayed in fanciful garments—had been able
to understand.

'But can't you see, Sammie, that those cool, cool trouserings
of yours are in fact a long, chenille, beige, off-the-shoulder, cut-
on-the-cross, low-backed gown? And that the exquisitely extraordinary thing round your neck is a necklace of pearls?'

'No,' Samantha had said.

As if he were mad. And those daughters, their big pale lips
revolving gum like cows at the cud, had glowered contempt.

Christ, he had thought, I've got three bloody wives to keep.

Three sets of lipsticks, eye-shadow, panties, tights, bras and all
the fearful rest. Quite a harem. Every week their sanitary arrangements alone cost him as much as a week's tobacco—but here he
caught himself, they were his wife and children, his nearest and
dearest, and more than that, the outward and visible sign of
the very inner settled state he prized.

At last a thrash of gates above! The hawsers moved into action,
the lift itself could be heard droning and rattling down.

The first sign of it was a long loop of wire, terribly loose-
looking against the bare concrete shaft-wall—where would it go
to underneath, was there room for it to coil, what *was* it anyway?
—and then the descending floor, and feet, and trousers, and two
staring zoo-faces at the grill. Rattling and pulling of catches and
doors. No good saying 'Got all day?' to them, it might provoke
an incident, delay things further—so he just glared an extra cold
'Thank you' to the man who held the door open, and left it to
clang automatically behind him.

But it did not. Bowlsend looked round at the irritating
apparatus—sometimes they closed themselves, sometimes not,
you never knew—but found another man on quiet feet had
arrived to share the lift with him, and was holding the door.

A quick appraisal, as Bowlsend made room for him. Man of
about his own age, blue suit, stripes too loud, briefcase, no hat,
glasses—he looked again, greyish glasses concealing eyes, the man
looked asleep.

'Floor?' asked Bowlsend, in charge of buttons.

'Top,' the man said. 'Five.'

'I'm four,' Bowlsend said, pressing the button, adding affably:
'Not quite so ambitious.'

The man smiled with his mouth, but the grey-glassed eyes
remained hooded; was this perhaps a cynical smile, marking him
one down for facetiousness? Defences arose, as the lift gave a
shudder and began the upwards pull.

They stood together at attention, upright as men together in a
urinal. Their eyes down at their feet for the first second: then
rising to briefcase level and up as far as the chest, when quickly
they switched to avoid each other's eyes—a meeting of eyes in
such an intimate mahogany box might compel speech. Speech
was unthinkable, the journey too short: the exchange of 'Nice

afternoon again' too obvious a nervous discharge. Besides, there was much to digest: from Bowlsend's instant survey, the man's bottom waistcoat button was done up, and his lapel winked a pinpoint red rosette—foreigner, perhaps? Extraordinary the impact of presence, even in such a short routine journey—invisible ectoplasms, waves of electric personality jetting everywhere. At least the man's glasses helped—you could not imagine being observed too closely through those occlusive lenses.

In any case, there was plenty to read: *Authorised Load Four Persons*. And the name of the maker of the lift embossed in rich-looking metal. And now—as their box encountered the first floor, a huge figure 1 painted on the concrete. Brief glimpse of an empty passageway through the grill, and they were hauled up and past like a very slow express train superior to unimportant stations. Was there a gravitational pull, Bowlsend wondered? The whole thing shuddered from time to time. As they climbed further, was the strain increased?

It was indeed very extraordinary to be suspended in what was really a little portable platform swaying on wires high above a deep dark well: nice of them to have furnished the thing so comfortably with reassuring mahogany panels, a mirror, a fluted glass shade haloing the little electric light. And now came floor 2, and a decided click as they passed. More well-wall, and oddly the feeling of ascending a ladder. Why? It was just the same as down below. The mind, Bowlsend, the bloody old mind picturing everything—better not think about it, have another look at this chap's midriff, see if you can spot his name on his briefcase . . . initials only, and anyway, why not addresses on briefcases? Are you supposed to lose them only on premises where your initials are known? Ridiculous.

Floor number 3, dragged past—next stop out. He looked down at his own briefcase, and quickly went over what he had to say in the office above. The lift stopped, and he reached out a hand to the gate.

'I shouldn't do that,' the other man's voice came, 'we're not exactly there.'

Bowlsend's eyes snapped up and on to blank concrete through the grill.

He controlled his voice: 'What's happened, then?'

'Ask me,' the man said.

At another time, Bowlsend might have grunted, 'I've just done so,' but not now, not now with his finger stabbing at button four and button four going in and out with no result whatever.

'Dead,' he said, regretting the word.

It was very quiet, the word echoed loud and hollow now that the mechanical hum had stopped. 'What do we do?' he added, as if it were rescuing them both back to life. 'Press this?' His finger poised itself over the red alarm button. Somewhere in the past he remembered hearing someone say, 'Never press it, it starts off all kinds of other stoppages.' Or was that not about the alarm, but the button marked Emergency Stop?

The man made a muttering sound of indecision. Then spoke as if he, too, disliked those out-of-the-way buttons: 'Ought to wait a minute or three, perhaps,' he said.

A minute or three—spreading on the nonchalance rather heavily? Cheering up the troops with a little joke? Play orchestra play! As ship and lift went down to the bottom, damn him.

'Give it *two* minutes, then,' Bowlsend said, flicking his watch out.

The man smiled. Again, with those clouded glasses, only with his mouth. A derisive smile?

'Might be here till Kingdom come,' he said, 'putting not too fine a limit on it.'

Ill-chosen phrase. But a casual one? Or was this a man of knowledge? Bowlsend stared at his little second-hand creeping round more slowly than he could ever have imagined. While his mind saw sudden clear pictures of a frayed hawser, the ends sticking up like the hairs of a metal brush, and only one thin steel tendon left on the wheel flange, its tensile strength strained to a final snap. Were there two hawsers? Where was the wheel? One downstairs, possibly for the counterweight, that huge thing flat as a giant corrugated black pillbox? Was there another wheel on the roof of their box? Safety devices, something clamping them automatically to a side girder? There *must* be such things. The authorities would insist. Like fire prevention. But then safety devices are themselves mechanised, could this go wrong too? And think of the amount of fires, in spite of all prevention laws . . .

As the little pointer went round he cursed himself for not knowing more of the mechanics of the thing. His car he could take to pieces and put together again. But lifts? Taken for granted. Absolute ignorance. Words like sheave, cam, flange flew about his mind, and alighted on nothing. There were overall conceptions like hydraulic: but at least, this was electric? A general power cut, then? That would be the most comfortable solution. Perhaps this other fellow knew more about it? Thinking this, Bowlsend felt sure the man did. For want of anyone else, the man automatically became a saviour. Despite his 'kingdom come'—or even now because of it. How hard the concrete looked, bare and ruthless, through the iron grill.

'What now?' Bowlsend said, as a minute was ticked up. 'Is there anything we can do?' It was a real query, he found himself appealing to this other chap as captain.

'As far as I can see,' the man drawled, 'which isn't all that far,' pointing a finger at the concrete well-wall, 'the only solution is a Greek one—a *deus ex machina*,* one might say.'

Christ, a bloody egg-head! Trapped with an egg-head—at this egg thought, frangibility zoomed, the egg was crushed and splattered all over the bottom of the shaft—and Bowlsend caught at himself, the man was at least taking it calmly.

'Well,' Bowlsend said, keeping his own voice calm, 'this is a pretty kettle of fish.'

'Indeed it is. You from the North, then?'

Bowlsend peered at the clouded glasses, now seeing huge eyes dimly magnified behind. And hairs, big hairs, magnified with the eyes.

'No—why?'

'Your expression—odd one, really.'

Was his face showing so much? Alarm, fear? But what impertinence!

'Kettle of fish,' the man went on, 'what does it mean? And why pretty?'

'Oh—I see. I've never really thought.'

This was absurd, with the alarm button and the emergency

*Providential intervention usually in literature.

button to attend to. Surely the 'stop' button needed a push for extra safety? Or would that invalidate anyone pressing some rescue button somewhere?

'Why I said North,' the man said, 'was because of the salmon. It's in point of fact a Scottish phrase. A kilted party would go out to fish the salmon and thereafter attempt an impromptu boil-up on the riverbank' Propelled by his reflections, the man dropped his position of attention, and took a couple of steps to one side, as if pacing in thought. The lift immediately swayed. Did it sway? It certainly shuddered, 'Which attempts resulted, often, in a pretty good mess-up.'

'I say, I shouldn't do that,' Bowlsend muttered.

'What?'

'Walk about. Might strain the thing.'

The man raised his eyebrows, they most visibly elevated themselves, two half circles above the clouds beneath. 'Oh?' he drawled.

'Don't really understand these things,' Bowlsend apologised; and then hopefully: 'But I expect you do?'

'Good heavens, no,' the man said, shocked at so mundane a thought. 'But let's consider those outside. The rescue team. It's mid-afternoon. A quarter to four. Absolutely tea-time, I'd say. Every blessed man-jack with his nose in a carton. Not forgetting every woman-jill. Could do,' he added casually, 'with a cup myself.'

So slowly he talked—then Bowlsend suddenly spotted it, a big watery bead of perspiration starting at the top of the man's forehead, just where the hair began. He was a fake! This casual drawl was all pretence. Or—perhaps discipline, the fiddler in the orchestra-pit sawing away with the scenery crashing down in flames? But the man was obviously under pressure. It had a stiffening effect on Bowlsend, the man was human, frail and afraid—it was up to Bowlsend to help him.

'Rescue team, eh?' He managed a laugh. 'Suppose in the last resort, the fire brigade comes and cuts us out of it, eh?' And immediately wished he had kept quiet, as the appalling sounds of sirens and bells occurred to him, the hissing of acetylene cutting gear, cups of tea handed down, blankets, doctors, morphine! He suddenly sprang at the gate, and pushed the handle further in—perhaps it had loosened, breaking the circuit, what circuit for God's sake? He pressed number 4 again. No result. But his footstep forward had given the lift another tremor, and itself made a sudden thump in all that silence. The thump seemed to sound right down the empty well beneath, the long dark drop.

'Sound as a bell, eh?' the voice drawled at his back. 'Let's try the whole ca-, as they say, -boodle.' And he reached forward and began to press button after button, floor after floor. 'In case it's your particular floor that's the trouble,' he muttered. Bowlsend felt a momentary resentment, *his* floor, of course, to blame—but said sharply, as no response came from any button, 'Better sound the alarm.'

The man had his finger poised on the red knob.

'Think so?' he asked. 'Sink or swim?'

For some reason, unformed but definite in both of them, it was still a questionable move.

'Why not?' Bowlsend said, finally.

'All right then' And the finger came down on the red button. And they listened. Bells should have clanged into action, surely even an echo from some caretaker's hole, some workroom with indicators, cups of tea, a bench, pin-ups?

Nothing. Dead, dead silence, somehow hollow.

There were now several new beads of sweat on the man's forehead. Bowlsend suddenly thought, what if he panics, what the hell if I'm trapped with a gibbering hysteric, ripping at the door, thumping about, banging on the panels? As with swimming, knock him out? Suppose I missed—the man might hit back, there'd be a fight?

Unthinkable. He raised his head suddenly, extending his throat bitternwise for booming, and boomed loud and clear: 'Hello! Hello, hell-o-o-o!'

From far above—or was it below?—a sly little voice answered: 'Hello. Hell-o-o-o'.

Little Sir Echo. That damned song, he thought, feeling now sick, really sick in his stomach. The echo had emphasised their utter loneliness.

'A-hoy! A-hoy up there!' the other man shouted. His voice was oddly high-pitched—hysteria? But he added as a pedantic surety:

'Down there!'

Again the echo repeated, dismal and lost, each word. A lost little soul crying—and Bowlsend suddenly saw again clearly the torn hawser and the huge ton-heavy counter-weight which must all the time be silently straining at it. Two weights, lift and counterweight, something had to break . . .?

And if it did? Smashing down in a second, a flash of blinding time, too sudden perhaps to notice—or is such a long second slowed down like a life-long film?—smashing dead on the sharp machinery in the pit below, sending the two of them where? Up against the roof. And Bowlsend slowly put his hands above his head and stood pretending he was smoothing his hair: then slowly bent down on one knee, as if to do a shoe-lace up—but his hands were on his head, he dragged one down to his shoe. If only that damned stripe-suit wasn't there, he'd curl up like a little ball in the corner. Balls bounce? He'd lie spreadeagled. No, he'd squat, muscles like springs.

Suddenly the sound of a door opening somewhere beneath and near. Voices. Footsteps echoing on the tiled floor. Somebody was leaving an office: '. . . you'll let me have those consignments invoiced separately? See you Thursday week, then . . .'

'Thursday week as ever was . . .'

Bowlsend drew a deep breath of thanks, but that other man was quicker, he bent down towards the space between the floor and the wall, and shouted:

'The lift's stuck!'

Voice now of a man speaking to himself: 'Blast, better walk down.' And then loud: 'Thanks!' A clatter of hurrying footsteps away down the stairs. And just below, a door shutting.

'Hey—below there!' the man yelled.

Bowlsend couldn't get his breath. At last he said:

'We! You left out *we*!'

'What?'

'You sounded like an engineer.' And suddenly he began banging on the mahogany panelling, sharp at first, then breaking down to a long rhythmic thump, thump, thump like a slow clap.

Between thumps the door beneath opened again. A voice called back into an office, 'Seem to be mending it,' and the door shut.

'Help!' yelled Bowlsend, too late. Help, sang the little voice far above—where? Among machinery, dead machinery, under a cold glass cupola?

The man drew out a handkerchief, began mopping the fear from his brow, caught Bowlsend's eye on him, and said, 'Getting hot, isn't it?'

Bowlsend's heart jumped. Hot? Just two bodies? An open grill? The dreadful suspicion came and he sniffed. Friction, fire? A red-hot casing somewhere smouldering into the wooden furnishings? He sniffed, his mind seeking smoke, and sure enough discerned a vague metallic tang in the air, not exactly smoke, not exactly hot oil, but what . . .?

It was only then that he realised he might never get out of it. And the regrets of conscience came, and unspoken words to a Power beyond—I'll do better, I'll be better to all of them, I'll drive them all out to that new marina. I'll see young Marlene gets her Family Planning on the Health. I'll put down a deposit on those tetrachromyl TV chairs Sammie wants . . . most of all, I'll be more *understanding*, they've got lives, thoughts, wishes, and oh heaven, we're pretty happy together, we'll make it a really happy household!

'He-e-lp!' boomed the stripe-suit, hauling in the word, beginning low, hauling up high to a shriek. Then again, again. Down and up, down and up. And the ceiling and the walls of the little cage closed in with the sound, it was a mere box they were shut in, an airless box with a hollow floor—Bowlsend's mind began to race, then he saw the man's breath could never last, so he joined in to help, and the two of them stood there howling like dogs shut in.

Nothing.

They both looked at each other breathless. Both tried to smile, crooked, downward smiles that instantly went.

'I'm no good on ladders,' the man suddenly said. 'Dizzy—'

'Ladders?'

'They might have to cut us out. Put a ladder down to the roof.'

'They?'

'Well—the—incidentally, do you know these offices well?'

'Not very.'

'Not ever seen anyone around? Kind of a caretaker, janitor?'

He saw a polished row of uniformed commissionaires in other offices. But not here. He racked his mind for an old man in a waistcoat, a spanner and a cup of tea in his gnarled, capable hands; but could remember none, the hall below was always bare, the lift stopped there basementless—that wheel, those damned plastic cartons. But perhaps there were steps to a basement? Lot of good that was, a man in an underground hole.

'No,' he said, 'I've never seen anyone.'

The man drew out a packet of cigarettes. 'Expect there'll be a night watchman,' he said in a low voice. He raised his eyebrows at the cigarette packet, counting the few left, and put it back in his pocket.

Night watchman? They would be there as long as that? That's if—he sniffed again, caught the metal tang again—they were still suspended up here. Perhaps even now, though the time they had already been there made it feel somehow firmer, the strain was silently massing?

'The people,' he said, 'have got to leave their offices later?'

'Perhaps,' the man said. 'But it's summer, they're short-staffed for holidays. And it's Friday. And there's a test match. God knows how many funerals they've cooked up, anyway Friday afternoon's become a sort of Saturday morning now there's no Saturday morning.'

'But you've got somebody above on the fifth?'

'I'm just delivering a contract. On my way home. Letter box, they said.'

'Good God! You mean—the whole week-end, then?'

The man said nothing.

But old Healey in the office he was going to visit? He'd surely be there. He began suddenly to shake. He saw Healey's face, the way it turned away any loaded question, Healey the dead-pan averter. Perhaps Healey, wanting to avoid the interview, had unintentionally-on-purpose already left? And was there something stone-walling about Healey's middle-aged many-cardiganed secretary, a woman all spectacles, grey hair made for a deaf-aid . . . hadn't he seen a plastic something by her ear, could it have been only the spectacles? No, too much, a deaf secretary— but as he avoided the thought, he remembered stories of how people had ceased to help in emergency nowadays, walked right by people lying on the pavement, scattered when there was any trouble . . . but here it was simpler, they only had to call that old chap in the basement, or the police? But even that would make them miss their trains . . .?

He was shaking hard now, he felt afraid, but not so afraid as this, it was a shaking he had heard about from people in the war, and after motor accidents, an uncontrollable shaking disconnected from mind. There were his hands, his knees—he looked down at them as things separate from him—shaking, shivering like a disease.

'You cold?' the man asked. 'Funny, I'm hot.' The big magnified eyes bored into him glaucously, finding him out.

'It's—it's claustrophobia,' he stammered, and as he said it the truth welled up enormously closing him in, the walls, the grill, the floor, the terrible ceiling, five walls and that iron thing, all pressing hard in, like a crowd in a tunnel, no space, no breath, and his own breath abruptly grew difficult, he breathed in and out quickly, gasping, as if he had been running, and he opened his mouth wide to give out a last despairing bellow for help, a sound broken by breathlessness into an awful long high-pitched scream, with the walls curving in black now, muzzed and dotted all round.

As if in answer, the lift gave a shudder.

Then quietly began to travel upwards.

Healey, he dimly saw, was standing by the gates of floor 4.

Wonderful, wonderful Healey . . . he'd get his two-and-a-half per cent now, even three!

The grill doors opened. Healey said: 'Why Bowlsend! I'd given you up!'

'We were s-s-s-stuck,' Bowlsend stammered, stepping quickly out, feeling the thing would fall away behind him.

'Me too,' came the stripe-suit's voice. 'I'm not staying in that confounded thing. Shanks's pony for the home run!' He looked much smaller out of the lift, platformed on the high wide passage. Had Bowlsend been slightly crouched all the time? And then to Bowlsend's astonishment the man opened his mouth in a first real laugh, and teeth sprouted everywhere, he had a whole mouthful of prominent horse-teeth stacked away, hidden all the time.

'Mmm,' Healey muttered at the lift, 'it *has* been a bit of a nuisance lately.'

Bit of a nuisance!

Healey was peering into the lift. 'But where's the lady? I thought I heard a woman—' then stopped himself, quickly looking at Bowlsend, ashamed of shaming him.

'Come on now,' he said. 'I expect you'd like a glass of water.'

Glass of water! Brandy, hot tea, blankets! The bastard was so matter-of-fact, so everyday. Or wood from the neck up—not a fraction over two per cent for him. Yet Bowlsend clung close behind him in his relief, and noticed with surprise how his own shaking had stopped; it had indeed been fear then, though somehow not consciously felt by the brain, at least not to the extent of shaking.

In the office, he sipped the water. Sipped, because his confusion told him men in from the desert sipped, a draught was too much for their racked stomachs.

'How long were you stuck for?' Healey asked.

'Oh, about—' and Bowlsend wondered, it seemed of course like an hour, but then he could check on his watch? 'About— well, a quarter of an hour,' he said with surprise.

'Long enough, I suppose,' Healey said with no feeling whatsoever, beginning to turn over papers.

'What in hell went wrong with the thing?'

Healey frowned at a document: 'Hmm, what? Oh, a circuit or something. Quite safe of course. They're attending to it.'

Bowlsend was about to burst with a 'Why the hell don't they put a Not Working notice up?' when be remembered his last piercing shout, and kept silent. He was so glad to be safe and out of the thing that his immediate relief put him a relaxed generous mood—that is, with anyone but Healey. Healey had heard that shout. He must be very cautious with Healey. So in the end Healey got his two-and-a-half per cent.

On the way home, Bowlsend called into the railway buffet and ordered himself a large brandy. An expensive drink, so he lingered over it and was late home.

By that time relief had expanded into pure strength. He felt bouncing fit, a man who triumphs over great odds. His last shout receded into a blinded past.

'Late?' he greeted Sammie. 'I should think so. Got stuck in a bloody lift. For an hour.'

'No,' he said at table to his assembled family, 'we are *not* going to the Wapham marina. Waste of time and money. It's time we all stiffened up a bit. Ought to be thankful we're alive, not spend the time always wanting more of this, more of that. And you Marlene, you're to be back home at eleven o'clock tonight. And every night, see?'

Suggestions for further reading

William Sansom wrote short stories throughout his career, and at least a dozen collections have been published. A wide-ranging selection edited by Elizabeth Bowen appeared in 1963 entitled *The Stories of William Sansom* published by The Hogarth Press. Subsequent volumes are: *The Ulcerated Milkman* (1966); *Hans Feet in Love* (1971), a series of stories relating the hero's amorous triumphs and failures leading up to his eventual marriage (cf Scott Fitzgerald's *Basil* stories and Maugham's *Ashenden* for other examples of cycles of short stories) and *The Marmalade Bird* (1973). Another facet of the conscious craftsmanship in Sansom's story-writing is revealed in *Lord Love Us* (1954), a collection of 'ballads' written in a kind of prose-verse.

Sansom also wrote eight novels of which the second, *The Face of Innocence* (1951), makes probably the most rewarding reading. The author explores his favourite theme of fantasy versus reality, or more precisely, the degree of illusion which is permissible in society. 'If an illusion injures the society around it, then it must be righted . . . sorted towards whatever illusion the society itself indulges in'. The heroine's dream world of travel and rich, kind uncles and the suffering it causes her friends excites some of Sansom's finest moments of tenderness and pathos (cf the story *A World of Glass* where a similar young woman, to all appearances perfectly normal, is eventually revealed to be suffering from a terrible disability). Sansom has also written five volumes of essays including *Pleasures Strange and Simple* (1953) and *Blue Skies, Brown Studies* (1961), a number of novellas or short novels and some juvenile fiction. Readers who are interested in the mechanical and imaginative processes of writing fiction are referred to *The Birth of a Story* published by Chatto and Windus in 1972, which gives an unusual insight into the author's method of writing as well as his views on the purpose and value of fiction.

Doris Lessing (born 1919)

Doris Lessing was born in Persia of British parents but she was taken to live on a farm in Southern Rhodesia at the age of five. Her career as a writer did not begin in earnest until the early nineteen-fifties by which time she had come to live in England. She has written a number of novels, several plays, a little poetry and some non-fiction, but like the other writers in this volume her most flawless achievements are her short stories. They do not however detract from the success of her first novel, *The Grass is Singing* (1950) or the acclaim which her highly original and experimental novel, *The Golden Notebook* (1962), has received. Doris Lessing is a compulsive story-writer, whether they are of novella length, as in *Five* (1953), with its opportunity for digression and a relaxed unfolding of the narrative, or the shorter, condensed tales in this selection. In her hands the genre becomes a supple and persuasive art form.

There is no set formula or pattern for a Doris Lessing story. Some are compressed life-histories; some concentrate on incidents which have a wider significance outside themselves; some are descriptive or reflective or both; some are written almost entirely in direct speech; two are letters; one is a report and so on. In addition to this variety of form there is an even greater range of interest and subject-matter. Nevertheless the stories do have one common characteristic—a pervasive seriousness. This is implicit in many of Doris Lessing's themes: the suffering and humiliation caused by the colour bar in Rhodesia; class conflicts in England; the claustrophobia and subterfuge within marriage; the problems of women living alone; *The Habit of Loving;* the trials and decisions of growing up. These aspects of life are laid bare with a courageous and refreshing honesty and the reader cannot but admire

Doris Lessing's sincerity and strength of conviction. She has an exceptional gift for psychological analysis and seems to understand instinctively why people behave as they do. This instinct combined with her descriptive powers accounts for the marked impact of many of the stories.

Doris Lessing's commitment to her subject is paramount: unlike Maugham she is not interested in writing simply to entertain the reader. She is rarely witty or amusing. After all she has spent half her life living in a country which she describes as 'the centre of a modern battlefield' and the remainder in a country which she must regard at times as alien. Except for such stories as *Pleasure* and possibly *England versus England,* where the humour is particularly pointed, the lighter touch is generally absent.

The influence of Africa on Doris Lessing's work is considerable. When after living in England she visited Rhodesia as a journalist, she was stimulated to write *Going Home* (1957) to record her anger at the feelings and the memories the visit revived. However, Africa also conferred a sense of the mystery of life and a rugged beauty which distinguishes *A Sunrise on the Veldt, The Old Chief Mshlanga* and *The Sun Between their Feet* amongst others. Doris Lessing writes: 'I believe the chief gift from Africa to writers, white or black, is the continent itself, its presence which for some people is like an old fever, latent always in their blood.' Against this background all man's problems and hardships can be seen in their true perspective. '. . . an almost full moon floated heavy and yellow above a stark granite-covered kopje. The bush around was black and low and silent, except that the crickets made a small incessant din' (from *The Story of Two Dogs*). In this landscape even the noise of crickets, normally loud and penetrating, is a 'small' sound.

Doris Lessing's African stories have been omitted from this selection since many of them have been widely anthologised already. Although *Flight* is set in Africa, the issues it deals with, the loneliness of an old man and the sadness of the moment when 'charming petulant spoiled children turn into serious young matrons', are universal and not specifically African. It is a beautiful and moving story which in the space of a few pages expresses the sorrow of lost innocence and passing youth, the mixed feelings with which one greets the new responsibilities of marriage and maturity and the loneliness of an old man whose pigeons now have to take the place of his grand-daughters in his affections. The story is a favourite of the author's and she should introduce it. 'Do I like it because I remember a very old man in a suburb in Africa, in a small house crammed with half-grown girls, all his life in his shelf of birds under jacaranda trees well away from that explosive house? In a green lacy shade he would sit and croon to his birds, or watch them wheel and speed and then come dropping back through the sky to his hand. The memory has something in it of a nostalgic dream' (from the Preface to *The Sun Between their Feet* (1973)). If it is the memory which accounts for the author's liking of the story, it is because she has succeeded in communicating its beauty and pathos that the story is admired by the reader.

The second story, *Notes for a Case History*, is in marked contrast to *Flight*. The reader's attention is held firmly at ground level by the more mundane matters of earning a living, courtship and 'getting on' generally. The story is written in the form of a dossier compiled on the early life of Maureen Watson including references to her best friend, Shirley, and her boyfriends. It is remarkable for its matter-of-fact analysis of the courtship game, how a young girl should use her 'capital', and the honest approach to the difficulties involved in moving from the working class to the middle class. Maureen takes all the right steps until she finally rebels on the crucial occasion of her fiancé's first meeting with her parents. It is then that the reader first admires her, but with this one gesture she loses all the advantage which she worked for so carefully.

The final story, *An Old Woman and Her Cat*, comes from Doris Lessing's latest collection published in 1972. It is one of her most powerful stories and is packed with such gall that the reader is made to wonder whether life in present-day England is any more civilised than that on the African veldt. The story of Hetty and Tibby illustrates the hardships of loneliness, poverty, widowhood, homelessness and the inadequacy and irrelevance of Welfare. Hetty and Tibby are as independent and self-sufficient as it is possible for people (and animals) in their position to be; they retain this but at what cost? Note Doris Lessing's use of detail throughout this story. Hetty is old, dirty and lonely but not unfeminine: '. . . the old woman's skirt, which today was cretonne curtain covered with pink and red roses that Hetty had pinned around her because she liked the pattern.' It is characteristic of Doris Lessing that in the last sentence of the story she should expose the euphemistic cliché, 'put him to sleep', thereby squeezing the last ounce of pathos from this harrowing tale.

Flight

Above the old man's head was the dovecote, a tall wire-netted shelf on stilts, full of strutting, preening birds. The sunlight broke on their grey breasts into small rainbows. His ears were lulled by their crooning, his hands stretched up towards his favourite, a homing pigeon, a young plumpbodied bird which stood still when it saw him and cocked a shrewd bright eye.

'Pretty, pretty, pretty,' he said, as he grasped the bird and drew it down, feeling the cold coral claws tighten around his finger. Content, he rested the bird lightly on his chest, and leaned against a tree, gazing out beyond the dovecote into the landscape of a late afternoon. In folds and hollows of sunlight and shade, the dark red soil, which was broken into great clods, stretched wide to a tall horizon. Trees marked the course of the valley; a stream of rich green grass the road.

His eyes travelled homewards along this road until he saw his grand-daughter swinging on the gate underneath a frangipani tree. Her fair fell down her back in a wave of sunlight, and her long bare legs repeated the angles of the frangipani stems, bare, shining-brown stems among patterns of pale blossoms.

She was gazing past the pink flowers, past the railway cottage where they lived, along the road to the village.

His mood shifted. He deliberately held out his wrist for the bird to take flight, and caught it again at the moment it spread its wings. He felt the plump shape strive and strain under his fingers; and, in a sudden access of troubled spite, shut the bird into a small box and fastened the bolt. 'Now you stay there,' he muttered; and turned his back on the shelf of birds. He moved warily along the hedge, stalking his grand-daughter, who was now looped over the gate, her head loose on her arms, singing. The light happy sound mingled with the crooning of the birds, and his anger mounted.

'Hey!' he shouted; saw her jump, look back, and abandon the gate. Her eyes veiled themselves, and she said in a pert neutral voice: 'Hullo, Grandad.' Politely she moved towards him, after a lingering backward glance at the road.

'Waiting for Steven, hey?' he said, his fingers curling like claws into his palm.

'Any objection?' she asked lightly, refusing to look at him.

He confronted her, his eyes narrowed, shoulders hunched, tight in a hard knot of pain which included the preening birds, the sunlight, the flowers, herself. He said: 'Think you're old enough to go courting, hey?'

The girl tossed her head at the old-fashioned phrase and sulked, 'Oh Grandad!'

'Think you want to leave home, hey? Think you can go running around the fields at night?'

Her smile made him see her, as he had every evening of this warm end-of-summer month, swinging hand in hand along the road to the village with that red-handed, red-throated, violent-bodied youth, the son of the postmaster. Misery went to his head and he shouted angrily: 'I'll tell your mother!'

'Tell away!' she said laughing, and went back to the gate.

He heard her singing, for him to hear:

'I've got you under my skin,
I've got you deep in the heart of . . .'

'Rubbish,' he shouted. 'Rubbish. Impudent little bit of rubbish!'

Growling under his breath he turned towards the dovecote, which was his refuge from the house he shared with his daughter and her husband and their children. But now the house would be empty. Gone all the young girls with their laughter and their squabbling and their teasing. He would be left, uncherished and alone, with that square-fronted, calm-eyed woman, his daughter.

He stooped, muttering, before the dovecote, resenting the absorbed cooing birds.

From the gate the girl shouted: 'Go and tell! Go on, what are you waiting for?'

Obstinately he made his way to the house, with quick, pathetic persistent glances of appeal back at her. But she never looked around. Her defiant but anxious young body stung him into love and repentance. He stopped. 'But I never meant . . .' he muttered, waiting for her to turn and run to him. 'I didn't mean . . .'

She did not turn. She had forgotten him. Along the road came the young man Steven, with something in his hand. A present for her? The old man stiffened as he watched the gate swing back, and the couple embrace. In the brittle shadows of the frangipani tree his grand-daughter, his darling, lay in the arms of the postmaster's son, and her hair flowed back over his shoulder.

'I see you!' shouted the old man spitefully. They did not move. He stumped into the little whitewashed house, hearing the wooden veranda creak angrily under his feet. His daughter was sewing in the front room, threading a needle held to the light.

He stopped again, looking back into the garden. The couple were now sauntering among the bushes, laughing. As he watched he saw the girl escape from the youth with a sudden mischievous movement, and run off through the flowers with him in pursuit. He heard shouts, laughter, a scream, silence.

'But it's not like that at all,' he muttered miserably. 'It's not like that. Why can't you see? Running and giggling, and kissing and kissing. You'll come to something quite different.'

He looked at his daughter with sardonic hatred, hating himself. They were caught and finished, both of them, but the girl was still running free.

'Can't you *see*?' he demanded of his invisible grand-daughter, who was at that moment lying in the thick green grass with the postmaster's son.

His daughter looked at him and her eyebrows went up in tired forbearance.

'Put your birds to bed?' she asked, humouring him.

'Lucy,' he said urgently. 'Lucy . . .'

'Well what is it now?'

'She's in the garden with Steven.'

'Now you just sit down and have your tea.'

He stumped his feet alternately, thump, thump, on the hollow wooden floor and shouted: 'She'll marry him. I'm telling you, she'll be marrying him next!'

His daughter rose swiftly, brought him a cup, set him a plate.

'I don't want any tea. I don't want it, I tell you.'

'Now, now,' she crooned. 'What's wrong with it? Why not?'

'She's eighteen. Eighteen!'

'I was married at seventeen and I never regretted it.'

'Liar,' he said. 'Liar. Then you should regret it. Why do you make your girls marry? It's you who do it. What do you do it for? Why?'

'The other three have done fine. They've three fine husbands. Why not Alice?'

'She's the last,' he mourned. 'Can't we keep her a bit longer?'

'Come, now, dad. She'll be down the road, that's all. She'll be here every day to see you.'

'But it's not the same.' He thought of the other three girls, transformed inside a few months from charming petulant spoiled children into serious young matrons.

'You never did like it when we married?' she said. 'Why not? Every time, it's the same. When I got married you made me feel like it was something wrong. And my girls the same. You get them all crying and miserable the way you go on. Leave Alice alone. She's happy.' She sighed, letting her eyes linger on the sun-lit garden. 'She'll marry next month. There's no reason to wait.'

'You've said they can marry?' he said incredulously.

'Yes, dad, why not?' she said coldly, and took up her sewing.

His eyes stung, and he went out on to the verandah. Wet spread down over his chin and he took out a handkerchief and mopped his whole face. The garden was empty.

From around a corner came the young couple; but their faces were no longer set against him. On the wrist of the postmaster's son balanced a young pigeon, the light gleaming on its breast.

'For me?' said the old man, letting the drops shake off his chin. 'For me?'

'Do you like it?' The girl grabbed his hand and swung on it. 'It's for you, Grandad. Steven brought it for you.' They hung about him, affectionate, concerned, trying to charm away his wet eyes and his misery. They took his arms and directed him to the shelf of birds, one on each side, enclosing him, petting him, saying wordlessly that nothing would be changed, nothing could change, and that they would be with him always. The bird was proof of it, they said, from their lying happy eyes, as they thrust it on him. 'There, Grandad, it's yours. It's for you.'

They watched him as he held it on his wrist, stroking its soft, sun-warmed back, watching the wings lift and balance.

'You must shut it up for a bit,' said the girl intimately. 'Until it knows this is its home.'

'Teach your grandmother to suck eggs,' growled the old man.

Released by his half-deliberate anger, they fell back, laughing at him. 'We're glad you like it.' They moved off, now serious and full of purpose, to the gate, where they hung, backs to him, talking quietly. More than anything could their grown-up seriousness shut him out, making him alone; also, it quietened him, took the sting out of their tumbling like puppies on the grass. They had forgotten him again. Well, so they should, the old man reassured himself, feeling his throat clotted with tears, his lips trembling. He held the new bird to his face, for the caress of its silken feathers. Then he shut it in a box and took out his favourite.

'*Now* you can go,' he said aloud. He held it poised, ready for flight, while he looked down the garden towards the boy and the girl. Then, clenched in the pain of loss, he lifted the bird on his wrist and watched it soar. A whirr and a spatter of wings, and a cloud of birds rose into the evening from the dovecote.

At the gate Alice and Steven forgot their talk and watched the birds.

On the veranda, that woman, his daughter, stood gazing, her eyes shaded with a hand that still held her sewing.

It seemed to the old man that the whole afternoon had stilled to watch his gesture of self-command, that even the leaves of the trees had stopped shaking.

Dry-eyed and calm, he let his hands fall to his sides and stood erect, staring up into the sky.

The cloud of shining silver birds flew up and up, with a shrill cleaving of wings, over the dark ploughed land and the darker belts of trees and the bright folds of grass, until they floated high in the sunlight, like a cloud of motes of dust.

They wheeled in a wide circle, tilting their wings so there was flash after flash of light, and one after another they dropped from the sunshine of the upper sky to shadow, one after another, returning to the valley and the shelter of night.

The garden was all a fluster and a flurry of returning birds. Then silence, and the sky was empty.

The old man turned, slowly, taking his time; he lifted his eyes to smile proudly down the garden at his grand-daughter. She was staring at him. She did not smile. She was wide-eyed, and pale in the cold shadow, and he saw the tears run shivering off her face.

Notes for a Case History

Maureen Watson was born at 93 Nelson's Way, N.1, in 1942. She did not remember the war. Or rather, when people said 'The War', she thought of Austerity: couponed curtains, traded clothes, the half-pound of butter swapped for the quarter of tea. (Maureen's parents preferred tea to butter.) Farther back, at the roots of her life, she *felt* a movement of fire and shadow, a leaping and a subsidence of light. She did not know whether this was a memory of a picture she had formed, perhaps from what her parents had told her of the night the bomb fell two streets from Nelson's Way and they had all stood among piles of smoking rubble for a day and night, watching firemen hose the flames. This feeling was not only of danger, but of fatality, of being helpless before great impersonal forces; and was how she most deeply felt, saw, or thought an early childhood which the social viewer would describe perhaps like this: 'Maureen Watson, conceived by chance on an unexpected granted-at-the-last-minute leave, at the height of the worst war in history, infant support of a mother only occasionally upheld (the chances of war deciding) by a husband she had met in a bomb shelter during an air-raid; poor baby, born into a historical upheaval which destroyed forty million people and might very well have destroyed her.'

As for Maureen, her memories and the reminiscences of her parents made her dismiss the whole business as boring, and nothing to do with her.

It was at her seventh birthday party she first made this clear. She wore a mauve organdie frock with a pink sash, and her golden hair was in ringlets. One of the mothers said: 'This is the first unrationed party dress my Shirley has had. It's a shame, isn't it?' And her own mother said: 'Well, of course these war children don't know what they've missed.' At which Maureen said: '*I* am not a war child,' 'What are you then, love?' said her mother, fondly exchanging glances. 'I'm Maureen,' said Maureen.

'And I'm Shirley,' said Shirley, joining cause.

Shirley Banner was Maureen's best friend. The Watsons and the Banners were better than the rest of the street. The Watsons lived in an end house, at higher weekly payments. The Banners had a sweets-paper-and-tobacco shop.

Maureen and Shirley remembered (or had they been told?) that once Nelson's Way was a curved terrace of houses. Then the ground floor level had broken into shops: a grocer's, a laundry, a hardware, a baker, a dairy. It seemed as if every second family in the street ran a shop to supply certain defined needs of the other families. What other needs were there! Apparently none; for Maureen's parents applied for permission to the Council, and the ground floor of their house became a second grocery shop, by way of broken-down walls, new shelves, a deep-freeze. Maureen remembered two small rooms, each with flowered curtains where deep shadows moved and flickered from the two small fires that burned back-to-back in the centre wall that divided them. These two rooms disappeared in clouds of dust from which sweet-smelling planks of wood stuck out. Strange, but friendly, men paid her compliments on her golden corkscrews and asked her for kisses, which they certainly did not get. They gave her sips of sweet tea from their canteens (filled twice a day by her mother) and made her bracelets of spiralling fringes of yellow wood. Then they disappeared. There was the new shop. Maureen's Shop. Maureen went with her mother to the sign-shop to arrange for these two words to be written in yellow paint on a blue ground.

Even without the name Maureen would have known that the shop was connected with hopes for her future; and that her future was what her mother lived for.

She was pretty. She had always known it. Even where the shadows of fire and dark were, they had played over a pretty baby. 'You were such a pretty baby, Maureen.' And at the birthday parties: 'Maureen's growing really pretty, Mrs Watson.' But all babies and little girls are pretty, she knew that well enough . . . no, it was something more. For Shirley was plump, dark—pretty. Yet their parents', or rather, their mothers' talk, had made it clear from the start that Shirley was not in the same class as Maureen.

When Maureen was ten there was an episode of importance. The two mothers were in the room above Maureen's Shop and they were brushing their little girls' hair out. Shirley's mother said: 'Maureen could do really well for herself, Mrs Watson.' And Mrs Watson nodded, but sighed deeply. The sigh annoyed Maureen, because it contradicted the absolute certainty that she felt (it had been bred into her) about her future. Also because it had to do with the *boring* era which she remembered, or thought she did, as a tiger-striped movement of fire. *Chance:* Mrs Watson's sigh was like a prayer to the Gods of Luck: it was the sigh of a small helpless thing being tossed about by big seas and gales. Maureen made a decision, there and then, that she had nothing in common with the little people who were prepared to be helpless and tossed about. For she was going to be quite different. She was already different. Not only the War, but the shadows of war had long gone, except for talk in the newspapers which had nothing to do with her. The shops were full of everything. The Banners' sweets-tobacco-paper shop had just been done up; and *Maureen's* was short of nothing. Maureen and Shirley, two pretty little girls in smart mother-made dresses were children of plenty, and knew it, because their parents kept saying (apparently they did not care how tedious they were) 'These kids don't lack for anything, do they, they don't know what it can be like, do they? This, with the suggestion that they ought to be grateful for not lacking anything, always made the children sulky, and they went off to flirt their full many-petticoated skirts where the neighbours could see them and pay them compliments.

Eleven years. Twelve years. Already Shirley had subsided into her rôle of pretty girl's plainer girl-friend, although, of course, she was not plain at all. Fair girl, dark girl, and Maureen by mysterious birthright was the 'pretty one', and there was no doubt in either of their minds which girl the boys would try first for a date. Yet this balance was by no means as unfair as it seemed. Maureen, parrying and jesting on street-corners, at bus stops, knew she was doing battle for two, because the boys she discarded, Shirley got: Shirley got far more boys than she would have done without Maureen who, for her part, needed, more—*had* to have a foil. Her rôle demanded one.

They both left school at fifteen, Maureen to work in the shop. She was keeping her eyes open: her mother's phrase. She wore a slim white overall, pinned her fair curls up, was neat and pretty in her movements. She smiled calmly when customers said: 'My word, Mrs Watson, your Maureen's turned out, hasn't she?'

About that time there was a second moment of consciousness. Mrs Watson was finishing a new dress for Maureen, and the fitting was taking rather long. Maureen fidgeted and her mother said: 'Well, it's your capital, isn't it? You've got to see that, love.' And she added the deep unconscious sigh. Maureen said: 'Well, don't go on about it, it's not very nice, is it?' And what she meant was, not that the idea was not very nice, but that she had gone beyond needing to be reminded about it; she was feeling the irritated embarrassment of a child when it is reminded to clean its teeth after this habit has become second nature. Mrs Watson saw and understood this, and sighed again; and this time it was the maternal sigh which means: Oh dear, you are growing up fast! 'Oh, *mum,*' said Maureen, 'sometimes you just make me tired, you do really.'

Sixteen. She was managing her capital perfectly. Her assets were a slight delicate prettiness, and a dress sense that must have been a gift from God, or more probably because she had been reading the fashion magazines since practically before consciousness. Shirley had put in six months of beehive hair, pouting scarlet lips, and an air of sullen disdain; but Maureen's sense of herself was much finer. She modelled herself on filmstars, but with an understanding of how far she could go—of what was allowable to Maureen. So the experience of being Bardot, Monroe, or whoever it was, refined her: she took from it an essence, which was learning to be a vehicle for other people's fantasies. So while Shirley had been a dozen stars, but really *been* them, in violent temporary transmogrifications, from which she emerged (often enough with a laugh) Shirley—plump, good-natured, and herself; Maureen remained herself through every rôle, but creating her appearance, like an *alter ego,* to meet the expression in people's eyes.

Round about sixteen, another incident: prophetic. Mrs Watson had a cousin who worked in the dress-trade, and this man, un-thought-of for many years, was met at a wedding. He commented on Maureen, a vision in white gauze. Mrs Watson worked secretly on this slender material for some weeks; then wrote to him: could Maureen be a model? He had only remote connections with the world of expensive clothes and girls, but he dropped into the shop with frankly personal aims. Maureen, in a white wrapper, was still pretty, very; but her remote air told this shrewd man that she would certainly not go out with him. She was saving herself; he knew that air of self-esteem very well from other exemplars. Such girls do not go out with middle-aged cousins, except as a favour or to get something. However, he told Mrs Watson that Maureen was definitely model material, but that she would have to do something about her voice. (He meant her accent, of course; and so Mrs Watson understood him.) He left addresses and advice and Mrs Watson was in a state of quivering ambition. She said so to Maureen: 'This is your chance, girl. Take it'. What Maureen heard was: 'This is *my* chance'.

Maureen, nothing if not alert for her Big Chance, for which her whole life had prepared her, accepted her mother's gift of £100 (she did not thank her, no thanks were due) and actually wrote to the school where she would be taught Voice Training.

Then she fell into sullen withdrawal, which she understood so little that a week had gone by before she said she must be sick—or something. She was rude to her mother: very rare, this. Her father chided her for it: even rarer. But he spoke in such a way that Maureen understood for the first time that this drive, this push, this family effort to gain her a glamorous future came from her mother, her father was not implicated. For him, she was a pretty enough girl, spoiled by a silly woman.

Maureen slowly understood she was not sick, she was growing up. For one thing: if she changed her 'voice' so as to be good enough to mix with new people, she would no longer be part of this street, she would no longer be *our Maureen*. What would she be, then? Her mother knew: she would marry a duke and be whisked off to Hollywood. Maureen examined her mother's ideas for her and shrank with humiliation. She was, above all, no fool, but she had been very foolish. For one thing: when she used her eyes, with the scales of illusion off them, she saw that the million streets of London blossomed with girls as pretty as she. What then had fed the illusion in herself and in other people? What accounted for the special tone, the special looks that always greeted her? Why, nothing more than that she, Maureen, because of her mother's will behind her, had carried herself from childhood as something special, apart, destined for a great future.

Meanwhile (as she clearly saw) she was in 93 Nelson's Way, serving behind the counter of Maureen's Shop. (She now wondered what the neighbours had thought—before they got used to it— about her mother's fondness so terribly displayed.) She was dependent on nothing less than that a duke or a film producer would walk in to buy a quarter or tea and some sliced bread.

Maureen sulked. So her father said. So her mother complained. Maureen was—thinking? Yes. But more, a wrong had been done her, she knew it, and the sulking was more of a protective silence while she grew a scab over a wound.

She emerged demanding that the £100 should be spent on sending her to Secretarial School. Her parents complained that she could have learned how to be a secretary for nothing if she had stayed on at school another year. She said: 'Yes, but you didn't have the sense to make me, did you? What did you think, I was going to sell butter like you all my life?' Unfair, on the face of it; but deeply fair, in view of what they had done to her. In their different ways they knew it. (Mr Watson knew in his heart, for instance, that he should never have allowed his wife to call the shop 'Maureen's'.) Maureen went, then, to Secretarial School for a year. Shirley went with her: she had been selling cosmetics in the local branch of a big chain-store. To raise the £100 was difficult for Shirley's parents: the shop had done badly, had been bought by a big firm; her father was an assistant in it. For that matter, it wasn't all that easy for the Watsons: the £100 was the result of small savings and pinching over years.

This was the first time Maureen had thought of the word capital in connection with money, rather than her own natural assets: it was comparatively easy for the Watsons to raise money, because they had capital: the Banners had no capital. (Mrs Watson said the Banners had had *bad luck*.) Maureen strengthened her will; as a result the two families behaved even more as if the girls would have different futures—or, to put it another way, that while the two sums of a hundred pounds were the same, the Watsons could be expected to earn more on theirs than the Banners.

This was reflected directly in the two girls' discussions about boys.

Shirley would say: 'I'm more easy-going than you'.

Maureen would reply: '*I* only let them go so far'.

Their first decisions on this almighty subject had taken place years before, when they were thirteen. Even then Shirley went further ('let them go further') than Maureen. It was put down, between them, to Shirley's warmer temperament—charitably; for both knew it was because of Maureen's higher value in the market.

At the Secretarial School they met boys they had not met before. Previously boys had been from the street or the neighbourhood, known from birth, and for this reason not often gone out with— that would have been boring. (Serious, with possibilities of marriage.) Or boys picked up after dances or at the pictures. But now there were new boys met day after day in the School. Shirley went out with one for weeks, thought of getting engaged, changed her mind, went out with another. Maureen went out with a dozen, chosen carefully. She knew what she was doing—and scolded Shirley for being so *soft*. 'You're just stupid, Shirley—I mean, you've got to get on, why don't you do like me?'

What Maureen did was allow herself to be courted, until she agreed at last, as a favour, to be taken out. First, lunch—a word she began to use now. She would agree to go out to lunch two or three times with one boy, while she was being taken out to

supper (dinner) by another. The dinner-partner, having been re-
warded by a closed-mouth kiss for eight, ten, twelve nights, got
angry or sulky or reproachful, according to his nature. He dropped
her, and the lunch partner was promoted to dinner partner.

Maureen ate free for the year of her training. It wasn't that she
planned it like this: but when she heard other girls say they paid
their way or liked to be independent, it seemed to Maureen
wrong-headed. To pay for herself would be to let herself be under-
valued: even the idea of it made her nervous and even sulky.

At the end of the training Maureen got a job in a big architects'
office. She was a junior typist. She stuck out for a professional
office because the whole point of the training was to enable her
to meet a better class of people. Of course she had already learned
not to use the phrase, and when her mother did snubbed her
with: 'I don't know what you mean, better *class*, but it's not much
point my going into that hardware stuck upstairs in an office by
myself if I can get a job where there's some life about.'

Shirley went into a draper's shop where there was one other
typist (female) and five male assistants.

In Maureen's place there were six architects, out most of the
time, or invisible in large offices visited only by the real secretaries;
a lower stratum of young men in training, designers, draughtsmen,
managers, etc.; and a pool of typists.

The young men were mostly of her own class. For some months
she ate and was entertained at their expense; and at each week-end
there was a solemn ceremony, the highpoint of the week, certainly
the most exciting moment in it, when she divided her wage. It
was seven pounds (rising to ten in three years) and she allocated
two pounds for clothes, four for the post office, and one pound
for the week's odd expenses.

At the end of a year she understood two things. That she had
saved something like £200. That there was not a young man in the
office who would take her out again. They regarded her, according
to their natures, with resentment or with admiration for her cool
management of them. But there was nothing doing *there*—so
they all knew.

Maureen thought this over. If she were not taken out to meals
and entertainment, she must pay for herself and save no money,
or she must never go out at all. If she was going to be taken out,

then she must give something in return. What she gave was an open mouth, and freedom to the waist. She calculated that because of her prettiness she could give much less than other girls.

She was using her *capital* with even more intelligence than before. A good part of her time—all not spent in the office or being taken out, went in front of her looking-glass, or with the better-class fashion magazines. She studied them with formidable concentration. By now she knew she could have gone anywhere in these islands, except for her voice. Whereas, months before, she had sulked in a sort of fright at the idea of cutting herself off from her street and the neighbours, now she softened and shaped her voice, listening to the clients and the senior architects in the office. She knew her voice had changed when Shirley said: 'You're talking nice, Maureen, much nicer than me.'

There was a boy in the office who teased her about it. His name was Tony Head. He was in training to be an accountant for the firm, and was very much from her own background. After having taken her out twice to lunch, he had never asked her again. She knew why: he had told her. 'Can't afford you, Maureen,' he said. He earned not much more than she did. He was nineteen, ambitious, serious, and she liked him.

Then she was nineteen. Shirley was engaged to one of the assistants in her shop, and would be married next Christmas.

Maureen took forty pounds out of her savings and went on a tour to Italy. It was her first time out of England. She hated it: not Italy, but the fact that half the sixty people on the tour were girls, like herself, looking for a good time, and the other half elderly couples. In Rome, Pisa, Florence, Venice, the Italians mooned over Maureen, courted her with melting eyes, while she walked past them, distant as a starlet. They probably thought she was one. The courier, a sharp young man, took Maureen out to supper one night after he had finished his duties, and made it clear that her mouth, even if opened, and her breasts, were not enough. Maureen smiled at him sweetly through the rest of the trip. No one paid her odd coffees, ices, and drinks. On the last night of the trip, in a panic because the £40 investment had yielded so little, she went out with an Italian boy who spoke seven words of English. She thought him crude, and left him after an hour.

But she had learned a good deal for her forty pounds. Quietly, in her lunch hour, she went off to the National Gallery and to the Tate. There she looked, critical and respectful, at pictures, memorizing their subjects, or main colours, learning names. When invited out, she asked to be taken to 'foreign' films, and when she got back home wrote down the names of the director and the stars. She looked at the book page of the *Express* (she made her parents buy it instead of the *Mirror*) and sometimes bought a recommended book, if it was a best-seller.

Twenty. Shirley was married and had a baby. Maureen saw little of her—both girls felt they had a new world of knowledge the other couldn't appreciate.

Maureen was earning £10 a week, and saved six.

There came to the office as an apprentice architect, Stanley Hunt, from grammar school and technical college. Tallish, well-dressed, fair with a small moustache. They took each other's measure, knowing they were the same kind. It was some weeks before he asked her out. She knew, by putting herself in his place, that he was looking for a wife with a little money or a house of her own, if he couldn't get a lady. (She smiled when she heard him using this word about one of the clients.) He tried to know clients socially, to be accepted by them as they accepted the senior architects. All this Maureen watched, her cool little face saying nothing.

One day, after he had invited a Miss Plast (Chelsea, well-off, investing money in houses) to coffee, and been turned down, he asked Maureen to join him in a sandwich lunch. Maureen thanked him delightfully, but said she already had an engagement. She went off to the National Gallery, sat on the steps, froze off wolves and pick-ups, and ate a sandwich by herself.

A week later, invited to lunch by Stanley, she suggested the Trattoria Siciliana which was more expensive, as she knew quite well, than he had expected. But this meal was a success. He was impressed with her, though he knew (how could he not, when his was similar?) her background.

She was careful to be engaged for two weeks. Then she agreed to go to the pictures—'a foreign film, if you don't mind, I think the American films are just boring.' She did not offer to pay, but remarked casually that she had nearly six hundred pounds in the post office. 'I'm thinking of buying a little business, some time. A dress shop. I've got a cousin in the trade.'

Stanley agreed that 'with your taste' it would be a sure thing.

Maureen no longer went to the Palais, or similar places (though she certainly did not conceal from Stanley that she had 'once') but she loved to dance. Twice they went to the West End together and danced at a Club which was 'a nice place'. They danced well together. On the second occasion she offered to pay her share, for the first time in her life. He refused, as she had known he would, but she could see he liked her for offering: more, was relieved; in the office they said she was mean, and he must have heard them. On that night, taken home lingeringly, she opened her mouth for him and let his hands go down to her thighs. She felt a sharp sexuality which made her congratulate herself that she had never, like Shirley, gone 'half-way' before. Well, of course girls were going to get married to just anybody if they let themselves be all worked up every time they were taken out!

But Stanley was not at all caught. He was too cool a customer, as she was. He was still looking for something better.

He would be an architect in a couple of years; he would be in a profession; he was putting down money for a house; he was good-looking, attractive to women, and with these assets he ought to do better than marry Maureen. Maureen agreed with him.

But, meanwhile, he took her out. She was careful often to be engaged elsewhere. She was careful always to be worth taking somewhere expensive. When he took her home, while she did not go so far as 'nearly the whole way', she went 'everything but'; and she was glad she did not like him better, because otherwise she would have been lost. She knew quite well she did not really like him, although her mind was clouded by her response to his hands, his moustache, his clothes and his new car.

She knew, because meanwhile a relationship she understood very well, and regretted, had grown up with Tony. He, watching this duel between the well-matched pair, would grin and drop remarks at which Maureen coloured and turned coldly away. He often asked her out—but only for 'a Dutch treat'—expecting her to refuse. 'How's your savings account, Maureen? I can't save, you girls get it all spent on you.' Tony took out a good many girls: Maureen kept a count of them. She hated him; yet she liked him, and knew she did. She relied on him above all for this grinning, honest understanding of her: he did not approve of her, but perhaps (she felt in her heart) he was right? During this period she several times burst into tears when alone, without apparent reason; afterwards she felt that life had no flavour. Her future was narrowing down to Stanley; and at these times she viewed it through Tony Head's eyes.

One night the firm had a party for the senior members of the staff. Stanley was senior, Maureen and Tony were not. Maureen knew that Stanley had previously asked another girl to go, and when he asked herself, was uncertain whether she could make it until the very last moment; particularly as his inviting her, a junior, meant that he was trying out on the senior members the idea of Maureen as his wife. But she acquitted herself very well. First, she was the best-looking woman in the room by far, and the best-dressed. Everyone looked at her and commented: they were used to her as a pretty typist; but tonight she was using all her will to make them look at her, to make her face and body reflect what they admired. She made no mistakes. When the party was over Stanley and two of the younger architects suggested they drive out to London airport for breakfast, and they did. The two other girls were middle class. Maureen kept silent for the most part, smiling serenely. She had been to Italy, she remarked, when a plane rose to go to Italy. Yes, she had liked it, though she thought the Italians were too noisy; what she had enjoyed best was the Sistine Chapel and a boat trip on the Adriatic. She hadn't cared for Venice much, it was beautiful, but the canals smelled, and there were far too many people: perhaps it would be better to go in winter? She said all this, having a right to it, and it came off. As she spoke she remembered Tony, who had once met her on her way to the National Gallery: 'Getting yourself an education Maureen? That's right, it'll pay off well, that will.'

She knew, thinking it all over afterwards, that the evening had been important for her with Stanley. Because of this, she did not go out with him for a week, she said she was busy talking to her cousin about the possibilities of a dress-shop. She sat in her room thinking about Stanley, and when thoughts of Tony came into her mind, irritatedly pushed them away. If she could succeed with Stanley, why not with someone better? The two architects from that evening had eyed her all the following week: they did not, however, ask her out. She then found that both were engaged to marry the girls they had been with. It was bad luck: she was sure that otherwise they would have asked her out. How to meet more like them? Well, that was the trouble—the drive to the airport was a bit of a fluke; it was the first time she had actually met the seniors socially.

Meanwhile, Stanley showed an impatience in his courtship—and for the first time. As for her, she was getting on for twenty-two, and all the girls she had grown up with were married and had their first or even their second babies.

She went out with Stanley to a dinner in the West End at an Italian restaurant. Afterwards they were both very passionate. Maureen, afterwards, was furious with herself: some borderline had been crossed (she supposed she still could be called a virgin?) and now decisions would have to be made.

Stanley was in love with her. She was in love with Stanley. A week later he proposed to her. It was done with a violent moaning intensity that she knew was due to his conflicts over marrying her. She was not good enough. He was not good enough. They were second-best for each other. They writhed and moaned and bit in the car, and agreed to marry. Her eight hundred pounds would make it easier to buy the house in a good suburb. He would formally meet her parents next Sunday.

'So you're engaged to Stanley Hunt?' said Tony.

'Looks like it, doesn't it?'

'Caught him—good for you!'

'He's caught me, more like it!'

'Have it your way.'

She was red and angry. He was serious.

'Come and have a bite?' he said. She went.

It was a small restaurant, full of office workers eating on luncheon vouchers. She ate fried plaice (no chips, please) and he ate steak-and-kidney pudding. He joked, watched her, watched her intently, said finally: 'Can't you do better than that?' He meant, and she knew it, better in the sense she would use herself, in her heart: he meant *nice*. Like himself. But did that mean that Tony thought *she* was nice? Unlike Stanley? She did not think she was, she was moved to tears (concealed) that he did. 'What's wrong with him, then?' she demanded, casual. 'What's wrong with *you*—you need your head examined.' He said it seriously, and they exchanged a long look. The two of them sat looking good-bye at each other: the extremely pretty girl at whom everyone in the room kept glancing and remarking on, and the good-looking, dark, rather fat accountant who was brusque and solemn with disappointment for her. With love for her? Very likely.

She went home silent, thinking of Tony. When she thought of him she needed to cry. She also needed to hurt him.

But she told her parents she was engaged to Stanley, who would be an architect. They would have their own house, in (they thought) Hemel Hempstead. He owned a car. He was coming to tea on Sunday. Her mother forgot the dukes and the film producers before the announcement ended; her father listened judiciously, then congratulated her. He had been going to a football match on Sunday, but agreed, after persuasion, that this was a good enough reason to stay home.

Her mother then began discussing, with deference to Maureen's superior knowledge, how to manage next Sunday to best advantage. For four days she went on about it. But she was talking to herself. Her husband listened, said nothing. And Maureen listened, critically, like her father. Mrs Watson began clamouring for a definite opinion on what sort of cake to serve on Sunday. But Maureen had no opinion. She sat, quiet, looking at her mother, a largish ageing woman, her ex-fair hair dyed yellow, her flesh guttering. She was like an excited child, and it was not attractive. *Stupid, stupid, stupid*—that's all you are, thought Maureen.

As for Maureen, if anyone had made the comparison, she was 'sulking' as she had before over being a model and having to be drilled out of her 'voice'. She said nothing but: 'It'll be all right, mum, don't get so worked up.' Which was true because Stanley knew what to expect: he knew why he had not been invited to meet her parents until properly hooked. He would have done the same in her place. He *was* doing the same: she was going to meet his parents the week after. What Mrs Watson, Mr Watson, wore on Sunday; whether sandwiches or cake were served; whether there were fresh or artificial flowers—none of it mattered. The Watsons were part of the bargain: what he was paying in return for publicly owning the most covetable woman anywhere they were likely to be; and for the right to sleep with her after the public display.

Meanwhile, Maureen had not said a word. She sat on her bed looking at nothing in particular. Once or twice she examined her face in the mirror, and even put cream on it. And she cut out a dress, but put it aside.

On Sunday Mrs Watson laid tea for four, using her own judgement since Maureen was too deeply in love (so she told everyone) to notice such trifles. At four Stanley was expected, and at 3.55 Maureen descended to the living-room. She wore: a faded pink dress from three summers before; her mother's cretonne overall used for housework; and a piece of cloth tied round her hair that might very well have been a duster. At any rate, it was a faded grey. She had put on a pair of her mother's old shoes. She could not be called plain; but she looked like her own faded elder sister, dressed for a hard day's spring-cleaning.

Her father, knowledgeable, said nothing: he lowered the paper, examined her, let out a short laugh, and lifted it again. Mrs Watson, understanding at last that this was a real crisis, burst into tears. Stanley arrived before Mrs Watson could stop herself crying. He nearly said to Mrs Watson: I didn't know Maureen had an older sister. Maureen sat listless at one end of the table; Mr Watson sat grinning at the other, and Mrs Watson sniffed and wiped her eyes between the two.

Maureen said: 'Hello, Stanley, meet my father and mother.' He shook their hands and stared at her. She did not meet his eyes: rather, the surface of her blue gaze met the furious, incredulous, hurt pounce of his glares at her. Maureen poured tea, offered him sandwiches and cake, and made conversation about the weather, and the prices of food, and the dangers of giving even good customers credit in the shop. He sat there, a well set-up young man, with his brushed hair, his brushed moustache, his checked brown cloth jacket, and a face flaming with anger and affront. He said nothing, but Maureen talked on, her voice trailing and cool. At five o'clock, Mrs Watson again burst into tears, her whole body shaking, and Stanley brusquely left.

Mr Watson said: 'Well, why did you lead him on, then?' and turned on the television. Mrs Watson went to lie down. Maureen, in her own room, took off the various items of her disguise, and returned them to her mother's room. 'Don't cry, mum, what

are you carrying on like that for? What's the matter?' Then she
dressed extremely carefully in a new white linen suit, brown
shoes, beige blouse. She did her hair and her face, and sat
looking at herself. The last two hours (or week) hit her, and her
stomach hurt so that she doubled up. She cried; but the tears
smeared her make-up, and she stopped herself with the side of
a fist against her mouth.

It now seemed to her that for the last week she had simply
not been Maureen; she had been someone else. What had she
done it for? Why? Then she knew it was for Tony: during all
that ridiculous scene at the tea-table, she had imagined Tony
looking on, grinning, but understanding her.

She now wiped her face quite clear of tears, and went quietly
out of the house so as not to disturb her father and mother.
There was a telephone booth at the corner. She stepped calm
and aloof along the street, her mouth held (as it always was) in
an almost-smile. Bert from the grocer's shop said: 'Hey,
Maureen, that's a smasher, who's it for?' And she gave him the
smile and the toss of the head that went with the street and said:
'You, Bert, it's all for you'. She went to the telephone booth
thinking of Tony. She felt as if he already knew what had
happened. She would say:' Let's go and dance, Tony'. He would
say: 'Where shall I meet you?' She dialled his number, and it
rang and it rang and it rang. She stood holding the receiver,
waiting. About ten minutes—more. Slowly she replaced it. *He
had let her down*. He had been telling her, in words and without,
to be something, to stay something, and now he did not care,
he had let her down.

Maureen quietened herself and telephoned Stanley.

Stanley answered, and she said amiably: 'Hello.'

Silence. She could hear him breathing, fast. She could see
his affronted face.

'Well, aren't you going to say anything?' She tried to make
this casual, but she could hear the fear in her voice. Oh yes, she
could lose him and probably had. To hide the fear she said:
'Can't you take a joke, Stanley?' and laughed.

'A joke!'

She laughed. Not bad, it sounded all right.

'I thought you'd gone off your nut, clean off your rocker . . .'

He was breathing in and out, a rasping noise. She was reminded of his hot breathing down her neck and her arms. Her own breath quickened, even while she thought: I don't like him, I really don't like him at all . . . and she said softly: 'Oh, Stan, I was having a bit of a giggle, that's all.'

Silence. Now, this was the crucial moment.

'Oh, Stan, can't you see—I thought it was all just boring, that's all it was.' She laughed again.

He said: 'Nice for your parents, I don't think.'

'Oh, they don't mind—they laughed after you'd left, though first they were cross.' She added hastily, afraid he might think they were laughing at him: 'They're used to me, that's all it is.'

Another long silence. With all her will-power she insisted that he should soften. But he said nothing, merely breathed in and out, into the receiver.

'Stanley, it was only a joke, you aren't really angry, are you, Stanley?' The tears sounded in her voice now, and she judged it better that they should.

He said, after hesitation: 'Well, Maureen, I just didn't like it, I don't like that kind of thing, that's all.' She allowed herself to go on crying, and after a while he said, forgiving her in a voice that was condescending and irritated: 'Well, all right, all right, there's no point in crying, is there?'

He was annoyed with himself for giving in, she knew that, because she would have been. He had given her up, thrown her over, during the last couple of hours: he was pleased, really, that something from outside had forced him to give her up. Now he could be free for the something better that would turn up—someone who would not strike terror into him by an extraordinary performance like this afternoon's.

'Let's go off to the pictures, Stan . . .'

Even now, he hesitated. Then he said, quick and reluctant: 'I'll meet you at Leicester Square, outside the Odeon, at seven o'clock.' He put down the receiver.

Usually he came to pick her up in the car from the corner of the street.

She stood smiling, the tears running down her face. She knew she was crying because of the loss of Tony, who had let her down. She walked back to her house to make up again, thinking

that she was in Stanley's power now: there was no balance
between them, the advantage was all his.

An Old Woman and Her Cat

Her name was Hetty, and she was born with the twentieth cen-
tury. She was seventy when she died of cold and malnutrition.
She had been alone for a long time, since her husband had died
of pneumonia in a bad winter soon after the Second World
War. He had not been more than middle-aged. Her four
children were now middle-aged, with grown children. Of these
descendants one daughter sent her Christmas cards, but otherwise
she did not exist for them. For they were all respectable people,
with homes and good jobs and cars. And Hetty was not respectable. She had always been a bit strange, these people said, when
mentioning her at all.

When Fred Pennefather, her husband, was alive, and the
children just growing up, they all lived much too close and uncomfortable in a Council flat in that part of London which is like
an estuary, with tides of people flooding in and out: they were
not half a mile from the great stations of Euston, St Pancras and
King's Cross. The blocks of flats were pioneers in that area,
standing up grim, grey, hideous, among many acres of little
houses and gardens, all soon to be demolished so that they could
be replaced by more tall grey blocks. The Pennefathers were good
tenants, paying their rent, keeping out of debt; he was a
building worker, 'steady', and proud of it. There was no evidence
then of Hetty's future dislocation from the normal, unless it was
that she very often slipped down for an hour or so to the platforms where the locomotives drew in and ground out again. She
liked the smell of it all, she said. She liked to see people moving
about, 'coming and going from all those foreign places'. She
meant Scotland, Ireland, and the North of England. These visits
into the din, the smoke, the massed swirling people, were for her
a drug, like other people's drinking or gambling. Her husband
teased her, calling her a gipsy. She was in fact part-gipsy, for her

mother had been one, but had chosen to leave her people and marry a man who lived in a house. Fred Pennefather liked his wife for being different from the run of the women he knew, and had married her because of it; but her children were fearful that her gipsy blood might show itself in worse ways than haunting railway stations. She was a tall woman with a lot of glossy black hair, a skin that tanned easily, and dark strong eyes. She wore bright colours, and enjoyed quick tempers and sudden reconciliations. In her prime she attracted attention, was proud and handsome. All this made it inevitable that the people in those streets should refer to her as 'that gipsy woman'. When she heard them, she shouted back that she was none the worse for that.

After her husband died and the children married and left, the Council moved her to a small flat in the same building. She got a job selling food in a local store, but found it boring. There seem to be traditional occupations for middle-aged women living alone, the busy and responsible part of their lives being over. Drink. Gambling. Looking for another husband. A wistful affair or two. That's about it. Hetty went through a period of, as it were, testing out all these, like hobbies, but tired of them. While still earning her small wage as a saleswoman, she began a trade in buying and selling second-hand clothes. She did not have a shop of her own, but bought or begged clothes from householders, and sold these to stalls and the second-hand shops. She adored doing this. It was a passion. She gave up her respectable job and forgot all about her love of trains and travellers. Her room was always full of bright bits of cloth, a dress that had a pattern she fancied and did not want to sell, strips of beading, old furs, embroidery, lace. There were street traders among the people in the flats, but there was something in the way Hetty went about it that lost her friends. Neighbours of twenty or thirty years' standing said she had gone queer, and wished to know her no longer. But she did not mind. She was enjoying herself too much, particularly the moving about the streets with her old perambulator, in which she crammed what she was buying or selling. She liked the gossiping, the bargaining, the wheedling from householders. It was this last which—and she knew this quite well of course—the neighbours objected to. It was the thin edge of the wedge.

It was begging. Decent people did not beg. She was no longer decent.

Lonely in her tiny flat, she was there as little as possible, always preferring the lively streets. But she had after all to spend some time in her room, and one day she saw a kitten lost and trembling in a dirty corner, and brought it home to the block of flats. She was on a fifth floor. While the kitten was growing into a large strong tom, he ranged about that conglomeration of staircases and lifts and many dozens of flats, as if the building were a town. Pets were not actively persecuted by the authorities, only forbidden and then tolerated. Hetty's life from the coming of the cat became more sociable, for the beast was always making friends with somebody in the cliff that was the block of flats across the court, or not coming home for nights at a time so that she had to go and look for him and knock on doors and ask, or returning home kicked and limping, or bleeding after a fight with his kind. She made scenes with the kickers, or the owners of the enemy cats, exchanged cat lore with cat-lovers, was always having to bandage and nurse her poor Tibby. The cat was soon a scarred warrior with fleas, a torn ear, and a ragged look to him. He was a multicoloured cat and his eyes were small and yellow. He was a long way down the scale from the delicately coloured, elegantly shaped pedigree cats. But he was independent, and often caught himself pigeons when he could no longer stand the tinned cat food, or the bread and packet gravy Hetty fed him, and he purred and nestled when she grabbed him to her bosom at those times she suffered loneliness. This happened less and less. Once she realised that her children were hoping that she would leave them alone because the old rag-trader was an embarrassment to them, she accepted it, and a bitterness that always had wild humour in it welled up only at times like Christmas. She sang or chanted to the cat: 'You nasty old beast, filthy old cat, nobody wants you, do they Tibby, no, you're just an alley tom, just an old stealing cat, hey Tibs, Tibs, Tibs.'

The building teemed with cats. There were even a couple of dogs. They all fought up and down the grey cement corridors. There were sometimes dog and cat messes which someone had to clear up, but which might be left for days and weeks as part of neighbourly wars and feuds. There were many complaints. Finally an official came from the Council to say that the ruling about keeping animals was going to be enforced. Hetty, like the others, would have to have her cat destroyed. This crisis coincided with a time of bad luck for her. She had had flu; had not been able to earn money; had found it hard to get out for her pension; had run into debt. She owed a lot of back rent, too. A television set she had hired and was not paying for attracted the visits of a television representative. The neighbours were gossiping that Hetty had 'gone savage'. This was because the cat had brought up the stairs and along the passageways a pigeon he had caught, shedding feathers and blood all the way; a woman coming in to complain found Hetty plucking the pigeon to stew it, as she had done with others, sharing the meal with Tibby.

'You're filthy,' she would say to him, setting the stew down to cool in his dish. 'Filthy old thing. Eating that dirty old pigeon. What do you think you are, a wild cat? Decent cats don't eat dirty birds. Only those old gipsies eat wild birds.'

One night she begged help from a neighbour who had a car, and put into the car herself, the television set, the cat, bundles of clothes, and the pram. She was driven across London to a room in a street that was a slum because it was waiting to be done up. The neighbour made a second trip to bring her bed and her mattress, which were tied to the roof of the car, a chest of drawers, an old trunk, saucepans. It was in this way that she left the street in which she had lived for thirty years, nearly half her life.

She set up house again in one room. She was frightened to go near 'them' to re-establish pension rights and her identity, because of the arrears of rent she had left behind, and because of the stolen television set. She started trading again, and the little room was soon spread, like her last, with a rainbow of colours and textures and lace and sequins. She cooked on a single gas ring and washed in the sink. There was no hot water unless it was boiled in saucepans. There were several old ladies and a family of five children in the house, which was condemned.

She was in the ground-floor back, with a window which opened on to a derelict garden, and her cat was happy in a hunting ground that was a mile around this house where his mistress was so splendidly living. A canal ran close by, and in the dirty city-water were islands which a cat could reach by leaping from moored boat to boat. On the islands were rats and birds. There were pavements full of fat London pigeons. The cat was a fine hunter. He soon had his place in the hierarchies of the local cat population and did not have to fight much to keep it. He was a strong male cat, and fathered many litters of kittens.

In that place Hetty and he lived five happy years. She was trading well, for there were rich people close by to shed what the poor needed to buy cheaply. She was not lonely for she made a quarrelling but satisfying friendship with a woman on the top floor, a widow like herself who did not see her children either. Hetty was sharp with the five children, complaining about their noise and mess, but she slipped them bits of money and sweets after telling their mother that 'she was a fool to put herself out for them, because they wouldn't appreciate it.' She was living well, even without her pension. She sold the television set and gave herself and her friend upstairs some day-trips to the coast, and bought a small radio. She never read books or magazines. The truth was that she could not write or read, or only so badly it was no pleasure to her. Her cat was all reward and no cost, for he fed himself, and continued to bring pigeons for her to cook and eat, for which in return he claimed milk.

'Greedy Tibby, you greedy *thing,* don't think I don't know, oh yes I do, you'll get sick eating those old pigeons, I do keep telling you that, don't I?'

At last the street was being done up. No longer a uniform, long, disgraceful slum, houses were being bought by the middle-class people. While this meant more good warm clothes for trading—or begging, for she still could not resist the attraction of getting something for nothing by the use of her plaintive inventive tongue, her still flashing handsome eyes—Hetty knew, like her neighbours, that soon this house with its cargo of poor people would be bought for improvement.

In the week Hetty was seventy years old, came the notice that was the end of this little community. They had four weeks to find somewhere else to live.

Usually, the shortage of housing being what it is in London— and everywhere else in the world, of course—these people would have had to scatter, fending for themselves. But the fate of this

particular street was attracting attention, because a municipal
election was pending. Homelessness among the poor was finding
a focus in this street which was a perfect symbol of the whole
area, and indeed the whole city, half of it being fine, converted,
tasteful houses, full of people who spent a lot of money, and
half being dying houses tenanted by people like Hetty.

As a result of speeches by councillors and churchmen, local
authorities found themselves unable to ignore the victims of this
redevelopment. The people in the house Hetty was in were
visited by a team consisting of an unemployment officer, a social
worker and a rehousing officer. Hetty, a strong gaunt old woman
wearing a scarlet wool suit she had found among her cast-offs that
week, a black knitted tea-cosy on her head, and black buttoned
Edwardian boots too big for her, so that she had to shuffle, invited them into her room. But although all were well used to the
extremes of poverty, none wished to enter the place, but stood in
the doorway and made her this offer: that she should be aided to
get her pension—why had she not claimed it long ago?—and that
she, together with the four other old ladies in the house should
move to a Home run by the Council out in the northern suburbs.
All these women were used to, and enjoyed, lively London, and
while they had no alternative but to agree, they fell into a sad-
dened and sullen state. Hetty agreed too. The last two winters
had set her bones aching badly, and a cough was never far away.
And while perhaps she was more of an urban soul even than the
others, since she had walked up and down so many streets with
her old perambulator loaded with rags and laces, and since she
knew so intimately London's texture and taste, she minded least
of all the idea of a new home 'among green fields'. There were,
in fact, no fields near the promised Home, but for some reason
all the old ladies had chosen to bring out this song of a phrase,
as if it belonged to their situation, that of old women not far off
death. 'It will be nice to be near green fields again,' they said to
each other over cups of tea.

The housing officer came to make final arrangements. Hetty
Pennefather was to move with the others in two weeks' time. The
young man, sitting on the very edge of the only chair in the
crammed room, because it was greasy and he suspected it had
fleas or worse in it, breathed as lightly as he could because of the

appalling stink: there was a lavatory in the house, but it had been out of order for three days, and it was just the other side of a thin wall. The whole house smelled.

The young man, who knew only too well the extent of the misery due to lack of housing, who knew how many old people abandoned by their children did not get the offer to spend their days being looked after by the authorities, could not help feeling that this wreck of a human being could count herself lucky to get a place in his Home, even if it was—and he knew and deplored the fact—an institution in which the old were treated like naughty and dim-witted children until they had the good fortune to die.

But just as he was telling Hetty that a van would be coming to take her effects and those of the other four old ladies, and that she need not take anything more with her than her clothes 'and perhaps a few photographs', he saw what he had thought was a heap of multicoloured rags get up and put its ragged gingery-black paws on the old woman's skirt. Which today was cretonne curtain covered with pink and red roses that Hetty had pinned around her because she liked the pattern.

'You can't take that cat with you,' he said automatically. It was something he had to say often, and knowing what misery the statement caused, he usually softened it down. But he had been taken by surprise.

Tibby now looked like a mass of old wool that has been matting together in dust and rain. One eye was permanently half-closed, because a muscle had been ripped in a fight. One ear was vestigial. And down a flank was a hairless slope with a thick scar on it. A cat-hating man had treated Tibby as he treated all cats, to a pellet from his airgun. The resulting wound had taken two years to heal. And Tibby smelled.

No worse, however, than his mistress, who sat stiffly still, bright-eyed with suspicion, hostile, watching the well-brushed, tidy young man from the Council.

'How old is that beast?'

'Ten years, no, only eight years, he's a young cat about five years old,' said Hetty, desperate.

'It looks as if you'd do him a favour to put him out of his misery,' said the young man.

When the official left, Hetty had agreed to everything. She was the only one of the old women with a cat. The others had budgerigars or nothing. Budgies were allowed in the Home.

She made her plans, confided in the others, and when the van came for them and their clothes and photographs and budgies, she was not there, and they told lies for her. 'Oh, we don't know where she can have gone, dear,' the old women repeated again and again to the indifferent van-driver. 'She was here last night, but she did say something about going to her daughter in Manchester.' And off they went to die in the Home.

Hetty knew that when houses have been emptied for re-development they may stay empty for months, even years. She intended to go on living in this one until the builders moved in.

It was a warm autumn. For the first time in her life she lived like her gipsy forbears, and did not go to bed in a room in a house like respectable people. She spent several nights, with Tibby, sitting crouched in a doorway of an empty house two doors from her own. She knew exactly when the police would come around, and where to hide herself in the bushes of the overgrown shrubby garden.

As she had expected, nothing happened in the house, and she moved back in. She smashed a back windowpane so that Tibby could move in and out without her having to unlock the front door for him, and without leaving a window suspiciously open.

She moved to the top back room and left it every morning early, to spend the day in the streets with her pram and her rags. At night she kept a candle glimmering low down on the floor. The lavatory was still out of order, so she used a pail on the first floor instead, and secretly emptied it at night into the canal which in the day was full of pleasure boats and people fishing.

Tibby brought her several pigeons during that time.

'Oh, you are a clever puss, Tibby, Tibby! Oh, you're clever, you are. You know how things are, don't you, you know how to get around and about.'

The weather turned very cold; Christmas came and went. Hetty's cough came back, and she spent most of her time under piles of blankets and old clothes, dozing. At night she watched the shadows of the candle flame on floor and ceiling—the

window-frames fitted badly, and there was a draught. Twice
tramps spent the night in the bottom of the house and she heard
them being moved on by the police. She had to go down to make
sure the police had not blocked up the broken window the
cat used, but they had not. A blackbird had flown in and had
battered itself to death trying to get out. She plucked it, and
roasted it over a fire made with bits of floorboard in a baking
pan: the gas of course had been cut off. She had never eaten very
much, and was not frightened that some dry bread and a bit of
cheese was all that she had eaten during her sojourn under the
heap of clothes. She was cold, but did not think about that very
much. Outside there was slushy brown snow everywhere. She
went back to her nest, thinking that soon the cold spell would be
over and she could get back to her trading. Tibby sometimes got
into the pile with her, and she clutched the warmth of him to
her. 'Oh, you clever cat, you clever old thing, looking after yourself, aren't you? That's right, my ducky, that's right, my lovely.'

And then, just as she was moving about again, with snow gone
off the ground for a time but winter only just begun, in
January, she saw a builder's van draw up outside, a couple of men
unloading their gear. They did not come into the house: they
were to start work next day. By then Hetty, her cat, her pram
piled with clothes and her two blankets, were gone. She also
took a box of matches, a candle, an old saucepan and a fork
and spoon, a tin-opener, and a rat-trap. She had a horror of rats.

About two miles away, among the homes and gardens of
amiable Hampstead, where live so many of the rich, the intelli-
gent and the famous, stood three empty, very large houses. She
had seen them on an occasion, a couple of years before, when she
had taken a bus. This was a rare thing for her, because of the
remarks and curious looks provoked by her mad clothes, and by
her being able to appear at the same time such a tough battling
old thing, and a naughty child. For the older she got, this dis-
reputable tramp, the more there strengthened in her a quality
of fierce, demanding childishness. It was all too much of a
mixture; she was uncomfortable to have near.

She was afraid that 'they' might have rebuilt the houses, but
there they still stood, too tumbledown and dangerous to be of
much use to tramps, let alone the armies of London's homeless.

There was no glass left anywhere. The flooring at ground level was mostly gone, leaving small platforms and juts of planking over basements full of water. The ceilings were crumbling. The roofs were going. The houses were like bombed buildings.

But in the cold dark of a late afternoon she pulled the pram up the broken stairs and moved cautiously around the frail boards of a second-floor room that had a great hole in it right down to the bottom of the house. Looking into it was like looking into a well. She held a candle to examine the state of the walls, here more or less whole, and saw that rain and wind blowing in from the window would leave one corner dry. Here she made her home. A sycamore tree screened the gaping window from the main road twenty yards away. Tibby, who was cramped after making the journey under the clothes in the pram, bounded down and out and vanished into neglected undergrowth to catch his supper. He returned fed and pleased, and seemed happy to stay clutched in her hard thin old arms. She had come to watch for his return after hunting trips, because the warm purring bundle of bones and fur did seem to allay, for a while, the permanent ache of cold in her bones.

Next day she sold her Edwardian boots for a few shillings—they were fashionable again—and bought a loaf and some bacon scraps. In a corner of the ruins well away from the one she had made her own, she pulled up some floorboards, built a fire, and toasted bread and the bacon scraps. Tibby had brought in a pigeon, and she roasted that, but not very efficiently. She was afraid of the fire catching and the whole mass going up in flames; she was afraid, too, of the smoke showing and attracting the police. She had to keep damping down the fire, and so the bird was bloody and unappetising, and in the end Tibby got most of it. She felt confused, and discouraged, but thought it was because of the long stretch of winter still ahead of her before spring could come. In fact, she was ill. She made a couple of attempts to trade and earn money to feed herself before she acknowledged she was ill. She knew she was not yet dangerously ill, for she had been that in her life, and would have been able to recognise the cold listless indifference of a real last-ditch illness. But all her bones ached, and her head ached, and she coughed more than she ever had. Yet she still did not think of herself as suffering particularly from the cold, even in that sleety January weather. She had never, in all her life, lived in a properly heated place, had never known a really warm home, not even when she lived in the Council flats. Those flats had electric fires, and the family had never used them, for the sake of economy, except in very bad spells of cold. They piled clothes on to themselves, or went to bed early. But she did know that to keep herself from dying now she could not treat the cold with her usual indifference. She knew she must eat. In the comparatively dry corner of the windy room, away from the gaping window through which snow and sleet were drifting, she made another nest—her last. She had found a piece of polythene sheeting in the rubble, and she laid that down first, so that the damp would not strike up. Then she spread her two blankets over that. Over them were heaped the mass of old clothes. She wished she had another piece of polythene to put on top, but she used sheets of newspaper instead. She heaved herself into the middle of this, with a loaf of bread near to her hand. She dozed, and waited, and nibbled bits of bread, and watched the snow drifting softly in. Tibby sat close to the old blue face that poked out of the pile and put up a paw to touch it. He miaowed and was restless, and then went out into the frosty morning and brought in a pigeon. This the cat put, still struggling and fluttering a little, close to the old woman. But she was afraid to get out of the pile in which the heat was being made and kept with such difficulty. She really could not climb out long enough to pull up more splinters of plank from the floors, to make a fire, to pluck the pigeon, to roast it. She put out a cold hand to stroke the cat.

'Tibby, you old thing, you brought it for me, then, did you? You did, did you? Come here, come in here . . .' But he did not want to get in with her. He miaowed again, pushed the bird closer to her. It was now limp and dead.

'You have it, then. You eat it. I'm not hungry, thank you, Tibby.'

But the carcass did not interest him. He had eaten a pigeon before bringing this one up to Hetty. He fed himself well. In spite of matted fur, and his scars and his half-closed yellow eye, he was a strong, healthy cat.

At about four the next morning there were steps and voices

downstairs. Hetty shot out of the pile and crouched behind a fallen heap of plaster and beams, now covered with snow, at the end of the room near the window. She could see through the hole in the floorboards down to the first floor, which had collapsed entirely, and through it to the ground floor. She saw a man in a thick overcoat and muffler and leather gloves holding a strong torch to illuminate a thin bundle of clothes lying on the floor. She saw that this bundle was a sleeping man or woman. She was indignant—*her* home was being trespassed upon. And she was afraid because she had not been aware of this other tenant of the ruin. Had he, or she, heard her talking to the cat? And where was the cat? If he wasn't careful he would be caught, and that would be the end of him! The man with a torch went off and came back with a second man. In the thick dark far below Hetty, was a small cave of strong light, which was the torchlight. In this space of light two men bent to lift the bundle, which was the corpse of a man or a woman like Hetty. They carried it out across the danger-traps of fallen and rotting boards that made gangplanks over the water-filled basement. One man was holding the torch in the hand that supported the dead person's feet, and the light jogged and lurched over trees and grasses: the corpse was being taken through the shrubberies to a car.

There are men in London who, between the hours of two and five in the morning, when the real citizens are asleep, who should not be disturbed by such unpleasantness as the corpses of the poor, make the rounds of all the empty, rotting houses they know about, to collect the dead, and to warn the living that they ought not to be there at all, inviting them to one of the official Homes or lodgings for the homeless.

Hetty was too frightened to get back into her warm heap. She sat with the blankets pulled around her, and looked through gaps in the fabric of the house, making out shapes and boundaries and holes and puddles and mounds of rubble, as her eyes, like her cat's, became accustomed to the dark.

She heard scuffling sounds and knew they were rats. She had meant to set the trap, but the thought of her friend Tibby, who might catch his paw, had stopped her. She sat up until the morning light came in grey and cold, after nine. Now she did know herself to be very ill and in danger, for she had lost all the warmth she had huddled into her bones under the rags. She shivered violently. She was shaking herself apart with shivering. In between spasms she drooped limp and exhausted. Through the ceiling above her—but it was not a ceiling, only a cobweb of slats and planks—she could see into a dark cave which had been a garret, and through the roof above that, the grey sky, teeming with incipient rain. The cat came back from where he had been hiding, and sat crouched on her knees, keeping her stomach warm, while she thought out her position. These were her last clear thoughts. She told herself that she would not last out until spring unless she allowed 'them' to find her, and take her to hospital. After that, she would be taken to a Home.

But what would happen to Tibby, her poor cat? She rubbed the old beast's scruffy head with the ball of her thumb and muttered: 'Tibby, Tibby, they won't get you, no, you'll be all right, yes, I'll look after you.'

Towards midday, the sun oozed yellow through miles of greasy grey cloud, and she staggered down the rotting stairs, to the shops. Even in those London streets, where the extraordinary has become usual, people turned to stare at a tall gaunt woman, with a white face that had flaming red patches on it, and blue compressed lips, and restless black eyes. She wore a tightly buttoned man's overcoat, torn brown woollen mittens, and an old fur hood. She pushed a pram loaded with old dresses and scraps of embroidery and torn jerseys and shoes, all stirred into a tight tangle, and she kept pushing this pram up against people as they stood in queues, or gossiped, or stared into windows, and she muttered: 'Give me your old clothes, darling, give me your old pretties, give Hetty something, poor Hetty's hungry.' A woman gave her a handful of small change, and Hetty bought a roll filled with tomato and lettuce. She did not dare go into a café, for even in her confused state she knew she would offend, and would probably be asked to leave. But she begged a cup of tea at a street stall, and when the hot sweet liquid flooded through her she felt she might survive the winter. She bought a carton of milk and pushed the pram back through the slushy snowy street to the ruins.

Tibby was not there. She urinated down through the hole in the boards, muttering, 'A nuisance, that old tea,' and wrapped herself in a blanket and waited for the dark to come.

Tibby came in later. He had blood on his foreleg. She had heard scuffling and she knew that he had fought a rat, or several, and had been bitten. She poured the milk into the tilted saucepan and Tibby drank it all.

She spent the night with the animal held against her chilly bosom. They did not sleep, but dozed off and on. Tibby would normally be hunting, the night was his time, but he had stayed with the old woman now for three nights.

Early next morning they again heard the corpse-removers among the rubble on the ground floor, and saw the beams of the torch moving on wet walls and collapsed beams. For a moment the torchlight was almost straight on Hetty, but no one came up: who could believe that a person could be desperate enough to climb those dangerous stairs, to trust those crumbling splintery floors, and in the middle of winter?

Hetty had now stopped thinking of herself as ill, of the degrees of her illness, of her danger—of the impossibility of her surviving. She had cancelled out in her mind the presence of winter and its lethal weather, and it was as if spring were nearly here. She knew that if it had been spring when she had had to leave the other house, she and the cat could have lived here for months and months, quite safely and comfortably. Because it seemed to her an impossible and even a silly thing that her life, or, rather, her death, could depend on something so arbitrary as builders starting work on a house in January rather than in April, she could not believe it: the fact would not stay in her mind. The day before she had been quite clear-headed. But today her thoughts were cloudy, and she talked and laughed aloud. Once she scrambled up and rummaged in her rags for an old Christmas card she had got four years before from her good daughter! In a hard harsh angry grumbling voice she said to her four children that she needed a room of her own now that she was getting on. 'I've been a good mother to you,' she shouted to them before invisible witnesses—former neighbours, welfare workers, a doctor. 'I never let you want for anything, never! When you were little you always had the best of everything! You can ask anybody, go on, ask them then!'

She was restless and made such a noise that Tibby left her and bounded on to the pram and crouched watching her. He was limping, and his foreleg was rusty with blood. The rat had bitten deep. When the daylight came, he left Hetty in a kind of sleep, and went down into the garden where he saw a pigeon feeding on the edge of the pavement. The cat pounced on the bird, dragged it into the bushes, and ate it all, without taking it up to his mistress. After he had finished eating, he stayed hidden, watching the passing people. He stared at them intently with his blazing yellow eye, as if he were thinking, or planning. He did not go into the old ruin and up the crumbling wet stairs until late—it was as if he knew it was not worth while going at all.

He found Hetty, apparently asleep, wrapped loosely in a blanket, propped sitting in a corner. Her head had fallen on her chest, and her quantities of white hair had escaped from a scarlet woollen cap, and concealed a face that was flushed a deceptive pink—the flush of coma from cold. She was not yet dead, but she died that night. The rats came up the walls and along the planks and the cat fled down and away from them, limping still, into the bushes.

Hetty was not found for a couple of weeks. The weather changed to warm, and the man whose job it was to look for corpses was led up the dangerous stairs by the smell. There was something left of her, but not much.

As for the cat, he lingered for two or three days in the thick shrubberies, watching the passing people and beyond them, the thundering traffic of the main road. Once a couple stopped to talk on the pavement, and the cat, seeing two pairs of legs, moved out and rubbed himself against one of the legs. A hand came down and he was stroked and patted for a little. Then the people went away.

The cat saw he would not find another home, and he moved off, nosing and feeling his way from one garden to another, through empty houses, finally into an old churchyard. This graveyard already had a couple of stray cats in it, and he joined them. It was the beginning of a community of stray cats going wild. They killed birds, and the field mice that lived among the grasses, and they drank from puddles. Before winter had ended the cats had had a hard time of it from thirst, during the two long spells when the ground froze and there was snow and no puddles and the birds were hard to catch because the cats were so easy to see against the clean white. But on the whole they managed quite well. One of the cats was a female, and soon there was a swarm of wild cats, as wild as if they did not live in the middle of a city surrounded by streets and houses. This was just one of half a dozen communities of wild cats living in that square mile of London.

Then an official came to trap the cats and take them away. Some of them escaped, hiding till it was safe to come back again. But Tibby was caught. Not only was he getting old and stiff—he still limped from the rat's bite—but he was friendly, and did not run away from the man, who had only to pick him up in his arms.

'You're an old soldier, aren't you?' said the man. 'A real tough one, a real old tramp.'

It is possible that the cat even thought that he might be finding another human friend and a home.

But it was not so. The haul of wild cats that week numbered hundreds, and while if Tibby had been younger a home might have been found for him, since he was amiable, and wished to be liked by the human race, he was really too old, and smelly and battered. So they gave him an injection and, as we say, 'put him to sleep'.

Suggestions for further reading

Doris Lessing's short stories have been published in several volumes and are conveniently available in paperback. *The Habit of Loving* (1957) and *A Man and Two Women* (1963) are two of the most varied collections dealing with such diverse subjects as the position of women, young and middle-aged, married and single, in modern society; the unhappy relationship between the working class and the middle class in England; the frustration of being a poet in a minority language; a plague of locusts; Rhodesian dung-beetles and many more. Mrs Lessing's latest collection is entitled *The Story of a Non-Marrying Man and Other Stories* (1972). The African stories have been collected and arranged into two volumes, *This Was the Old Chief's Country* and *The Sun Between Their Feet* both published by Michael Joseph. These volumes also contain the five novellas originally published in *Five* (1953), which won the Somerset Maugham award for 1954.

The success of Doris Lessing's first novel, *The Grass is Singing* (1959), was fully deserved and the book has lost none of its relevance today. It describes the gradual disintegration of an admittedly rather shaky marriage, which would probably have survived had it not been for the social and political difficulties of living with poverty and the colour bar on an isolated Rhodesian farm. The novel is economically written and has an urgency and single-mindedness which is very reminiscent of the short stories. The later novels have been more diffuse and have dealt with such subjects as the struggles of the communist party in Africa; mental breakdown and the inadequacy of medical treatment available; the problems and inner feelings of modern women and the breakdown of civilised society, the latter category verging on science fiction. *In Pursuit of the English* (1961), which records Doris Lessing's impressions of England after living here for ten years, provides further evidence of her powers of objective description.

Some Topics for Discussion

F. Scott Fitzgerald

The Jelly-Bean
1. Jim Powell is a Jelly-bean; Clark Darrow is 'one of the best beaux in the town'. Why are they still friends?
2. Nancy Lamar has a selfish, destructive element in her character which eventually catches up with her. Why is she universally liked? Why is she attracted to Jim?
3. Explain the sentence: 'He had been her moral laundry; the stains were his'. (page 20)
4. What do you learn of the American South from this story?

Outside the Cabinet-Maker's
1. What are the man's feelings towards his daughter during their conversation?
2. 'The King and Queen and Prince were killed and now the Princess is queen.' Is there any relationship between the family and the characters in the fairy tale?
3. What is the significance of the final paragraph of the story?

What a Handsome Pair!
1. What is Teddy's opinion of Stuart?
2. Compare the characters of Betty and Helen. What qualities does Teddy find attractive in each woman?
3. Which marriage is in your opinion more successful?

W. Somerset Maugham

The Lotus Eater
1. What does the author find intriguing about Thomas Wilson?
2. Find all the references to the moon in the story. What effect do they have on the narrative?
3. If you were in Wilson's place would you have made the same decision?

The Escape
1. There are two reasons for Roger's unusual method of breaking off his engagement. What are they and how far do they justify his subsequent actions?

Winter Cruise
1. Explain the change that occurs in Captain Erdmann's feelings (and those of his crew) for Miss Reid during the cruise.
2. The author explains in his preface to *Creatures of Circumstance*—1947 that he has resisted the temptation to change the nationality of the ship's crew in spite of the attitude to the Germans after the Second World War. How much of the humour is dependent upon national characteristics?
3. What is *your* opinion of Miss Reid?

William Sansom

My Little Robins
1. Why is the author's attention held by the engineer?
2. Although very purposeful, the engineer's behaviour is equally illogical. Try to account for his actions.
3. One major element of the description in this story is the use of colour. (Re-read the story noting the references to colour.) What else do you notice about the descriptive writing?

Eventide
1. Sansom conveys the atmosphere of the bar with a series of significant details. Give examples of some of these and describe their effectiveness.
2. All the sounds in the bar are magnified by the intervening silence. Give examples of some of them and analyse the handling of dialogue in this story.

Where Liberty Lies
1. Explain Rodney's attitude to women.
2. The demands of regular employment have been replaced for Rodney by other pressures. What are they?
3. What is your attitude to eccentrics like Rodney?
4. What is *your* idea of 'Liberty'?

The Day the Lift . . .

1. The reader is given a very full account of Mr Bowlsend during his monologue while he waits for the lift. How would you describe him? What are his major preoccupations?
2. What are the main differences between Bowlsend and his fellow traveller?
3. How does the reader know that the two men are becoming more and more afraid?
4. What effect does this experience have on Mr Bowlsend's subsequent behaviour?

Doris Lessing

Flight

1. During the story the old man's sorrow moves him to tears. At the end he is smiling proudly and his grand-daughter is crying. Account for this change.
2. The old man is the central figure in the story. Describe your feelings towards him.

Notes for A Case History

1. Maureen and Shirley manage their 'capital' in different ways. Which way appeals to you?
2. Why did Maureen behave as she did when Stanley came to her parents' house for tea?
3. What are the major differences between Stanley and Tony? Should Maureen have settled for Stanley or would she have been happier with Tony?

An Old Woman and Her Cat

1. What qualities do Hetty and Tibby have in common?
2. To what extent is Hetty responsible for her own fate?
3. Imagine you are the housing officer. Describe your visit to Hetty's home and outline your feelings towards her.
4. Compare this story with *Old Man Alone* by William Sansom, which deals with the same subject.

Acknowledgements

The Author and Publishers wish to thank the following for permission to use copyright material: The Bodley Head for *The Jelly-Bean* and *Outside the Cabinet-Maker's* from *The Bodley Head Scott Fitzgerald* and for *What a Handsome Pair!* from *Bits of Paradise* by F. Scott Fitzgerald; The Estate of W. Somerset Maugham and William Heinemann Ltd for *The Escape, The Man from Glasgow, The Lotus Eater*, and *Winter Cruise* from *The Complete Short Stories of W. Somerset Maugham*; William Sansom for *My Little Robins* and *Eventide* from *The Stories of William Sansom*, published by the Hogarth Press, © William Sansom 1963, for *The Day the Lift . . .* from *The Marmalade Bird* by William Sansom, published by the Hogarth Press, © William Sansom 1973, for *Where Liberty Lies* from *The Vertical Ladder and Other Stories* by William Sansom, published by Chatto & Windus Educational, © William Sansom 1966; Doris Lessing for *Notes for a Case History* from *A Man and Two Women*, for *Flight* from *The Sun between their Feet* and for *The Old Woman and Her Cat* from *The Story of a Non-Marrying Man* by Doris Lessing.